Dating After Forty-Eight

Morgan K Wyatt

Published by Sleeping Dragon

Copyright © October 2015
Print Edition

Cover by Dawne Dominique

To obtain permission to excerpt portions of the text, please contact the
author at morgankwyatt@gmail.com.

ISBN: 978-0-9966411-0-4

www.morgankwyatt.com
www.facebook.com/AuthorMorganKWyatt

Contents

Introduction

WHY WRITE A BOOK ABOUT dating after forty-eight? I had a co-worker who had never married, and she often regaled us with stories of having a better chance of dying in a terrorist attack, than actually meeting an eligible man. Strange, since my co-worker was an intelligent, attractive, professional woman with a wicked sense of humor. Why hadn't she found a companion?

Many of us rush through life in a desperate panic to find *The One*. Some people warn against looking for someone special and instead recommend settling for someone you can tolerate. In fact, a recent survey revealed that at least twenty-five percent of men marry women they do not love. These same men admit not even being attracted to their spouse. Why?

Dating, romance, and love are work. It seems like too much work for too little payoff, especially if you've suffered through a divorce or endured failed relationships. What if you could learn from a variety of experts? I have combed through endless dating books, watched videos and joined online dating sites. I even had a matchmaker and a dating coach.

My goal was to meet a better quality of men. My old approach to dating was to date anyone who asked me out; being stuck in a female-heavy profession left me with few opportunities. Since I wanted to meet someone appropriate,

I decided to take a scientific approach. With that in mind, I recorded my observations and results via a blog journal. More than 151,000 people have viewed the blog.

My dating journey involved discarding ideas I once regarded as truths. This allowed me to meet several high-quality men. Naturally, I didn't click with all of them, but I did find someone who was perfect for me. Twice married, I know the difference between settling and being with the perfect person for me. I want others to be able to experience the same happiness. To that end, I combined my fifty-one most popular blogs. With luck and effort, you may find your own sweetie.

I went back and added to my original blogs. The italicized sections are updates to the original blog. It is more of me explaining the reason behind the blog or blog order. At the end of the blogs may be a summary. Often, I now have more information than when I wrote the blog.

Avoiding the Romance Scam

I think we all have wondered…when a relationship falls flat or our home equity or bank account is depleted in the name of love, why give romance another try? This is probably why **Avoiding the Romance Scam** *is one of my most read blog posts. I chose this as my opening chapter since I do not want anyone to waste time on someone who is only using you. People will play you for a place to live, for a meal ticket, for a job in your company, for medical benefits, and for money.*

WHO DOESN'T HOPE THAT CUPID aims his arrow your way, especially if he has already targeted a likely sweetheart? Often, it isn't Cupid targeting you. Nefarious types have been using romance as a lure to land lovelorn men and women for centuries. This isn't a new game either, but the rules differ somewhat according to gender.

How do you avoid being a target? Watch where you meet people. Surprisingly, more women have confidence in online dating service eHarmony for the mere fact that it charges more. Surely, only a man with a serious interest in dating would lay out the monthly fee. It also offers the option to confirm your identity. Free dating sites tend to attract the amateur scam artists who can practice their romantic cons at no cost. Beware of men whose writing skills are limited and their English is odd. There are many foreign con men tricking women out of their money.

Is your guy writing beautiful, lyrical poetry to you?

Maybe you are suspicious of him or the poem. You can look it up on Google by including the words in quotes. This allows you to see what song or poem it belonged to originally. Is the guy too handsome to be true in his photo? You can send his photo through www.tineye.com to see if the picture has been copied from an image online. I found it easier just to show the image to friends, though. A friend identified a profile picture of my lyrical sweetheart as an NFL quarterback.

In some cons, the smitten boyfriend delivers several letters worthy of a romance writer. Unfortunately, countries separate them, but he is doing his best to get by her side if she could only wire him some money until his money clears Customs, or some other foreign currency-related issue is resolved.

Another twist on this is the soldier lover. He may really be a soldier, but I doubt it. He needs money to get home. Ladies, the government, flies them home free of charge when their tour is finished. My son is in the military. He has never paid any type of fee to come back. This fraud uses the good name of the United States Army. Don't send that money; you'll never see your uniformed Romeo because he is not overseas. In fact, he may not exist.

The female scammer goes for the long game most of the time. Many women actually view the more socially challenged men as meal tickets. Men should never to put their annual salary on their profiles. You have gold-digging honeys shopping for the lonely high-wage earner. She'll be sweet before the marriage and become your worst nightmare after the wedding. A smart man should dump this gold digger, but she knows how to work the man. Often, she'll quit her job, making herself dependent. How can he throw her out when she has no place to go? She'll use her children, his insecurities, even threats of committing suicide if he leaves her. Run, men, run! How do you know she's a gold digger?

Is she very interested in your income? Can she quote the current Kelley Blue Book value of your car? Does she always name expensive venues for dates and expects elaborate gifts? If so, you've a gold digger on your hands. She doesn't want you. She wants your paycheck. No, she will not kill herself because that would make it much harder to spend your money.

Another way we make ourselves targets is by casually giving away information. I had a good friend who is very frugal. One day at work, she announced she had saved thirty thousand dollars for a down payment on a house. I was impressed because she worked two modest jobs. Apparently, she mentioned it to several people because a liquid eyed lothario suddenly appeared in her life.

A man, whom no one knew, romanced her and asked to borrow her money for a business venture. The money and the fast-talking boyfriend disappeared immediately. The difference between the male con is that he usually comes in quick and takes a large sum of money and vanishes, while the female leech will continue to suck the man dry for extended periods of time.

Don't share your troubles. Conniving con artists are looking for someone with a recent loss, such as a relationship breakup, a death in the family, or even the death of a pet. Anything that has you off-kilter and not thinking straight offers them a chance to swoop in to comfort you.

Under normal circumstances, you might not look at the man or woman twice, but suddenly they're your rock. Even though friends might warn you off this trickster, you explain how wrong they are since the trickster helped you over a bad patch. What the trickster really did was worm his way into your affections while scrutinizing your checking account and your medical plan.

A co-worker going through a divorce inadvertently gave away her ATM number to a boyfriend who conveniently cleaned out her account right before Christmas. The comforting behavior this ne'er-do-well displayed was grooming to obtain the information he needed. This is exactly what pedophiles do to children to gain their trust.

How do you avoid being a target? Date people that are within driving range. Be suspicious. If a date doesn't feel or sound right, drop him. I've gone out on many dates, and at least fifty percent were wrong for one reason or another. Is someone asking questions about things they shouldn't, such as details about your income, your medical plan, your ability to have children in the future? If so, leave fast. Do not reveal where you live or your last name until you feel safe. You'd be amazed the information you can get online by knowing only a person's full name and hometown. Be careful what you give out on your social network sites, too.

After a close friend of mine had died, a man who knew I was vulnerable approached me. He obtained this information from one of my social media sites, which was marked "friends only." Even sites you think are private are not as private as you think. People can play you when you don't listen to your gut. We try to be nice to everyone. Don't. If you feel uneasy about a person or situation, move on. Once you suspect you're in a con, drop all contact. You owe this person nothing. Any communication will continue the con. You don't have time for this type of nonsense.

Defining What You Want

*Ever wonder why you dated people that weren't right for you?
This is something you realize in hindsight after you've invested
months, even years, in a relationship that was mediocre at best.
You can't get what you want if you don't know what it is you
want.*

DID YOU KNOW MORE WOMEN initiate divorce than men do?
The reason is they married a man they thought was right for
them, but later on, found out differently. Often, women
enter relationships without knowing exactly what they want
in a man. Men tend to be more precise. If you are going
shopping, it is better to know what you're looking for so you
don't bring home someone who doesn't fit.

Here it is the New Year, and I failed to make my man-
shopping list, which might be a bad thing. It depends.
According to Arielle Ford, life coach and author of **Mani-
festing the Love of your Life with the Law of Attraction**, if I
don't develop my intention about what type of man I desire,
then who knows who I'll attract to me? It may be the wrong
type. I could have made the list. I started to, but burning it
and finding a body of water to release the ashes on was too
much work.

Considering that I would have had to sneak out under
the cover of night and cross a private, snowy field to get to a
body of water; my ideal man might be dressed in blue with a
gun strapped to his hip. I'm not against a man in uniform,

but I would like to meet under less felonious conditions.

Marie Forleo, author of **Make Every Man Want You**, advises against a list. She finds that you tend to overlook men who could be wonderful, but don't exactly fit the list. Often, our lists are composed of things we deemed valuable at sixteen. Dreamy, brown eyes are not a requirement for me anymore. I think that was because of a teen heartthrob I was in love with at the time. Should looks matter?

This is a struggle. If I say they do, I sound, well…like a man. If I say they don't, most of you would call me a liar. We like certain physical types, but that type may not be the right one for us. I'm guilty of being a reactionary. If I dated a big, muscle-bound, he-man type for the last year, I'm definitely not in the market for another. Some women look for certain physical traits, such as a deep voice and a tight butt. As for me, I like revealing eyes and clean hands. Odd combination, I know.

The eyes tell me so much if I am willing to gaze deep. The eyes are the windows to the soul. The hands tell what the eyes don't. It doesn't matter what a man does for a living; any man can keep his hands clean and his nails clipped. Dirty, ragged nails are an instant turnoff. While many women are checking out a man's backside, I am checking out his hands.

Hair used to be big for me since I have excellent hair. Maybe I wanted a thick-haired man so we could toss our heads around as if in a shampoo commercial. My old preference of luxuriantly maned men changed after a couple dates with bald men and men who shaved their heads. Bald men can be scorching. Consider that at least twenty-five percent of men suffer from male-pattern baldness. Do I really want to eliminate that twenty-five percent? The percentage is actually higher in my age group. Besides excellent eyes and clean hands, what else matters on the outside?

Personally, I want men who manage to look both calm and content. There is an air of serenity about them. They look happy. Give me a pass on the angry, intense-looking men. Definitely not my style. I used to like the artistic-looking types. You know the ones, soulful eyes, overlong hair, and artistic clothing combinations. They liked me because they could smell job and health plan a mile away. Like fast food, they were something I gave up to improve my quality of life.

Instead, I went with one of my favorite interior characteristics: brains. How I love an intelligent man! I could gush all over the place about this, but he needs to be quietly intelligent, balanced with a sense of humor. An understated, dry sense of humor works well with significant intellect. Some guys are determined to prove how intelligent they are...that's just not smart. No one likes that. I seek out brainy men, which can be done by profession. When I decided I wanted a smart and stable guy, my first thought was an engineer. My best friend teases me that I have an engineer dating profile, but I do like them...a lot. They are so much better than my previous type, which was anyone who would ask me out.

I felt obligated to go out with the wrong men because of some misunderstood, motherly advice about being nice to every guy who asked me out. I am concerned about being physically fit and used to manage an aerobics studio. I went out with men whose exercise routines consisted of searching for the remote. I don't expect my dates to be cut, but I would like them to be active. My inactive dates weren't that much fun. Another couch potato might love the idea of snuggling up for endless hours of television, but not me.

Some things I want in a man are intangible. For instance, I want a male who is a hard worker, responsible, but at the same time open to adventure. A man who respects himself and what he does, but doesn't take himself too seriously. I know this is the type of talk we women do that drives men wild…and not in a good way. I want a man who will dance in the rain with me or take off for a weekend road trip. I want a paradox. Probably that man doesn't exist, but I believe he does. In fact, I think there are thousands of single male paradoxes out there. Maybe they are even feeling misunderstood because they don't fit into any category.

Finally, I want a man with a sense of play. Life can be deadly serious. Why make it more so? A man with playful manner can break away from the expected from time to time, even if those moments are private. A whimsical nature can be as small as challenging each other to a foot race or as far-fetched as devising elaborate treasure hunts where the ultimate prize could be very interesting. I think women would be much more playful if men made the first step. Older women like to comment that all men are just big children, but they usually say it with a smile, meaning they often like it even if they pretend they don't. Don't get me wrong. I want the whole package.

If I had a classified ad, it would read: *Wanted: Single, intelligent man with a stable career and personality (read: mentally healthy). Must be reasonably fit with interests besides watching television and surfing the Net. He must have a sense of humor, a spirit of adventure and a streak of playfulness. Beautiful eyes and hands are not required, but would be nice to have. Absolutely must love dogs.*

Okay, ladies, I guess I did make a list. I do have an intention. According to Ford, the life coach, that should draw the man to me. The fact that I even put it online should make the draw so much stronger...or so I think. Well, do you have a list? What's on it?

Update: *Did I get that man with all the characteristics I wanted? Yes, I did. I am amazed he existed, but I couldn't find him until I defined what I wanted.*

Online Dating / Can't Buy Me Love

You don't bump into single, appropriate folks every day. The older you are, the less likely you are to flirt with a cute guy in the dairy section. That brings me to online dating.

WELL...MAYBE I CAN AT least find out if there are likely men in the area. That's my first thought, as another commercial comes on featuring a smiling couple who met online. Let's face it. It's Friday night, and I am alone at home watching a Seinfeld marathon. Besides, the online site is having a free trial period. If I'm quick, I can snag a man without even joining. That's my plan...along with several thousand plus other people.

According to the US Census, there are more single adults in the United States than married people. With those type of numbers, why be alone on Friday night? I do wonder if they counted the men in prison, mental institutions, and on life support. If so, that actually decreases the numbers, but still I grab the laptop. I know the drill. I'm no online dating novice. Those photos when you initially open the site of people in your city do not live in your city. I haven't seen them anywhere.

The smooth-faced males with soulful eyes, garbed in tailored clothing would stand out among the grizzled, tired men in NASCAR jackets in my town. I did see them on the promos for various other dating sites. That's because the smaller sites are interconnected. You might sign up with

Hottiesbeus.com and suddenly you are receiving mail and offers from maturehotties.com and singlehotties.com. (I made up the names, but they might become real sites.) The joining fee is only about thirty dollars to join the initial group, but you only receive a few appropriate matches. There is the thought of joining another add-on group to increase your odds. Resist. You pay for the same pool of men. The big companies who can afford commercials offer you more possibilities.

Knowing what I know, I signed up with the granddaddy of dating sites for my free trial. I have ten days—that sounds like a lot, but it isn't. There is the initial processing (who knows what goes on there) before your matches arrive. The matches come without photos, making it hard to decide.

Everyone knows men tend to be attracted to a woman's outward appearance. As a female, I like to think I'm not that shallow, but I would like a photo. That gives me a hint. A man who can't even manage a smile for a dating website is not someone who would attract me. Better yet, (I am joking here) is the man holding an oversized margarita in a bar. I would definitely pass on the man posing with the Hooters' girls. Photos tell us so much, especially the pictures a man picks to interest a potential date. Unfortunately, the free trial doesn't offer photos.

All I have to go on is a few words on a profile. Words he may not have written. Daughters, sisters, even mothers have written profiles for the men in their lives. I even offered to write a profile for an ex-boyfriend. I do find some profiles that interest me, and I send a wink or a comment. Be cautious; some of the low-end sites allow you to Instant Message the person immediately. Often IMing is used by men already in relationships for a thrill, to check the waters, or even as a game when a bunch are together. You may not be IMing the man whose photo you saw in the profile because you'll never actually meet him. Know whom you are talking to. This becomes a bit tricky.

I've overheard high school students talking about creating profiles online. Of course, they tried to create a profile that met their teenage fantasies. It must have represented a great deal of older male fantasies also because they got a lot of hits. They used a photo from the Swedish Bikini Ski Team. It was a great game for them to respond to letters from lovelorn men. I mention this because online daters need to be careful.

Use a nickname instead of your real name; be vague about where you live, say a nearby town, but not yours. As a newbie, I used my name, the exact small suburb of a larger city where I lived, and I had a picture of my giant monstrosity of a dog and me. The result was a match (I rejected) started following me around town yelling my name. I joked that I had to move to get away from my stalker, but I did move. Watch what you reveal. It's better not to say anything messy online.

Please be careful of the too good to be real men. They write beautifully and if you actually paid for a membership, you'll see their extreme hotness factor. The shock of all shocks, they're interested in you. Your wonderful online friend thinks you might be soulmates…it is almost like a romantic novel. Don't spend too much time on this one because he's not real and will be asking you for money soon. Been there, did that. I didn't send money, but I did send the somewhat familiar photo to my friends. They recognized him as an NFL quarterback, which meant the sender was bogus. Back to the actual men, or what I think are real men.

Okay, I sent off a few nods and winks to guys I might be interested in. I also got a few back. Now is the time to exchange the stilted questions. I make fun of these, but in truth what do you really say when talking to someone you don't know. If I were good at this, I wouldn't be online! Some reply, some don't. One or two that respond might say something weird. The pool of matches just got significantly smaller. This isn't going as well, or as quick, as I expected. Work and life clog up my free time when I could be online. My trial is running out as the company is quick to remind me. It takes almost six months (they cheerfully point out) to find the right one. Each time I login, they flash their join-up now price, which is still too high.

On the last day of the trial, they drop their price about seventy-five percent. I join because they cut their prices and there were a few guys I just wanted to know better. I was curious what they looked like and I wanted to continue to get to know them.

Update: *Looking back on this whole process, I found out a few things about dating sites. Free sites offered men who weren't serious about finding a companion. They wanted to hang out when it was convenient for them. They often thought of themselves as players. It is also where people in a relationship shop.*

Developing Your Online Profile

This section is from articles I wrote for Examiner, as a local dating reporter.

ARE YOU TIRED OF THE roller coaster world of online dating, hitting mainly valleys, and none of the peaks? Could be you have a lackluster profile. You are charming, upbeat, even fun, but your profile doesn't show it.

Many online books promise eye-catching profiles, with the expert help being questionable at best. One book advised men to top their profiles with weird, cryptic titles such as: "Where Are My Sunglasses? Oh, Here They Are." Cheesy pickup lines as catchphrases are mind-numbingly painful. Intelligent women see those and keep looking.

Ask your friends what they like best about you. Tell them you are writing a profile, and you'll be amazed what they come up with. Men ask your women friends or sisters who are well aware that the ability to throw a perfect spiral is not dating profile material.

Here are five proven tips for writing an excellent profile.

1. Remember to stay positive. Do not drag out baggage.
2. Embrace your uniqueness; that way you stand out from the crowd.
3. Make sure you include something everyone likes to do, such as eating. If you list pole vaulting, ultra-

marathons, and geocaching as your go-to items, you will limit your possibilities.

4. Be descriptive. While you don't have to overwhelm with words, the right words pack more punch as opposed to generalities.

5. Stay current. If your profile includes the latest movie, book, or restaurant you visited, make sure you update it at least once a month. Otherwise, it looks like you are doing nothing new. It is a bit like real estate; the updated and newer listings get more looks.

Keep in mind, your unique sense of humor or sarcasm may not read well. The reader can't hear your tone of voice or see your twisted smile to be aware you're teasing. It is okay to be clever, but don't try too hard because it shows.

Here is an example of a thought-provoking heading: *Looking for My Last First Date.* The reader has to pause for a moment to understand the person wants a long-term relationship. The moment the reader stops to think, his or her interest is tickled. That's all you need to gain a second glance.

People, especially women, read the profiles. Don't dash this off in a hurry because you need to sound intelligent. Check your grammar and spelling so you don't come off as illiterate.

Over three-quarters of people lie on their profile to make themselves sound more attractive. Some lies will only cause you grief as opposed to getting you a second date.

1. Lying about your height is a big one – Sure, some women only want to date taller men. Then there are men who only want to date shorter women.

2. Marital status is the biggest one. If you're separated,

but going through a divorce, admit it. It will cut out the people who do not want to date a separated individual

3. Saying you want a long-term relationship when you don't. Often men, and sometimes women, make up excuses about getting back with an ex to keep a relationship from becoming too serious. Be up front with your intentions, and you should find someone like-minded.

4. Photo lies – Please use recent pictures, both close-ups, and full lengths. No Photo Shopped images or glamour shots.

5. Most people inflate their salaries – Be honest, there are people definitely looking for a meal ticket, so why pretend to be it. **Then again, why mention it.**

6. Pretending to be Bi – Some women think this makes them sound hot. What they get are guys who expect them to be bi-sexual and open to a threesome.

7. The kids misrepresentation – This works two ways. You pretend you don't have children when you do, or you have no interest in having kids when you do.

8. Pretending not to smoke or drink – How long is this going to last, especially if you hit it off.

9. Your geographical location – Women should never give specific addresses for safety. Often people state they live in high profile places when they don't.

10. The love of animals when one doesn't – Why lie to attract a dog lover when he or she come with a dog.

11. Pretending to like sports when you don't – You might find yourself scaling a cliff when you are deathly afraid of heights because of an untruth.

12. Ivy League education pretense – Most people don't care where your degree came from. Those who do can often check only using search engines.

13. My faith is everything – People pretend to have deep religious beliefs to pick up church girls or guys.

14. Languages and the ability to speak several feels safe until your date tries to talk to you in a foreign language.

15. Saying you aren't interested in physical appearance when you are – You can emphasize you are an avid athlete and are looking for a like-minded person if looking for a lean body type.

16. You're a fan of the arts – The problem is your date will want to go to the opera, symphony, and ballet.

There are probably more, but these seem to be the major ones put in profiles to attract dissimilar people. By lying, you waste both yours and the other person's time. Sadly, you probably decrease your chance of meeting someone you would connect with by lying about who you really are.

Photo Op

THIS IS WHERE MOST OF the complaints come from when people bitterly complain about their online dates looking nothing like their profile pic. Everyone wants to look good on their profile but using a photo where you are twenty years younger or fifty pounds lighter isn't fair to you or your date. You'll end up attracting men or women who want the younger, lighter version of you. When you show up, they're mad, which makes for a bad date.

People who might like the current you bypass your photo because they figure you wouldn't like them because they happen to look their age. Different sites tell you different things you should do for a photo.

The first thing you need to do is take some current photos of you by yourself. Close-ups, full lengths, doing something active, and remember to smile.

Men Do's & Don'ts

- Use pictures of you only. A trio of your golf buddies could have your date imagining one of them as her date only to be disappointed when you show up.
- Dress well. This is your first impression. No shirt unbuttoned to your navel, ratty shorts, or speedos.
- Don't use a picture of yourself with another woman, even your daughter. A woman wants to imagine herself by your side.

- Do ask a friend to take photos of you or go to a professional. The selfies or bathroom pictures show a lack of initiative.
- Show candid photos of yourself doing something you love from playing with the dog to barbecuing.
- Don't use photos with identifying information on them such as your work logo in the background.
- Don't take pictures of you and your car, motorcycle or boat. This is cheesy and all you get is a woman who wants to date your car, motorcycle, or boat.
- Avoid holding beer or a drink. While you may mention you drink on your profile, you do not want to give the appearance of always drinking.

One site suggested holding a baby. I would strongly advise against this. Women in their forties don't want to raise your child or grandchild. I never responded to any man who was holding a baby in his photos.

Women Do's & Don'ts

- Look good, but avoid Photo Shopping your images. You'll never be able to recreate this look and your date will be disappointed.
- Have full-length photographs. It is okay if you're not thin. Standing shows you to your advantage, anyhow.
- Take photos outside with greenery and blue skies. This has a positive effect on the man viewing the photo.
- Dress in a flattering manner, but not provocative. The cleavage show scares away your conservative and religious men. It also scares off men looking for a life

partner. All you are left with is men hoping to hook up.

- Avoid any alcoholic drink in your hand to avoid looking like a party girl.
- Do not take photos with children or grandchildren. The children can attract pedophiles. Children under twenty-one, aren't supposed to be in the pictures.
- Men and women have different senses of humor. The photo in your Charlie Chaplin costume will not be funny to men. Avoid strange outfits, clown noses, or anything else you might find gut-busting funny.
- You love your cats, but leave them out of the picture. Same goes for small dogs, especially dressed in costumes. A big dog can be a plus in a photo.
- Your goal is to look like yourself. Make sure you smile, even if you don't generally. If you pull off not looking like a deranged serial killer, then you've done much better than many.

The Confidence Game

THE FIRST STEP TO DATING like a Bond character is self-confidence. Act as if you are the most beautiful person in the room. Anyone should be glad to know you. If they aren't anxious to meet you, then that's their loss. I know some of you are shaking your heads, thinking that you could never pull this off. I did say ACT. That's the secret. Fake it until you make it. Why act self-confident if you're not feeling it?

Neediness is the opposite of confidence and drives men and women away. A woman lacking self-confidence telegraphs desperation. She feels like she can never land a man, so she dates anyone who asks her out. Then she usually sleeps with the guy on the first date since that is all she thinks she has to offer. She immediately begins to text, email, and call. Maybe she buys him gifts and drops them off at his work or home. No wonder the guy runs off screaming, which confirms her belief that she has nothing to offer. A worse scenario is the guy hangs around and uses the woman. He keeps her in place by insulting her, making her think she can't do better.

When we see men swarming around a woman, we make up stories why men are attracted to her without knowing the real reasons. First, she dresses like a slut. The second is she IS a slut. That somehow eases our mind about her appeal. Some of you might think. "I don't want to attract all the guys, just one special one." I'm with you on that, but the same thing that attracts every other red-blooded man will still attract that one particular male. It's not the fishnet stockings coupled with black leather mini-skirts. Sure, men look—we women look. However, women usually say something like, "OMG, she goes out in public like that." or "Wonder where I can get that skirt?"

To be a poised woman, you have to embrace that you are enough right now. Too many women believe a man or the loss of another ten pounds will make them happy—not true. The decision to live in the moment makes the difference. Accept yourself where you're at. Pursue interests you've always wanted to and believe in yourself. Face your fears head on.

My fear was that I would become a lonely, old woman with cats. First, I'm not a cat person. Second, I'm somewhat involved, so I don't spend a great deal of time alone. Age is relative. I met men much younger than me who seemed much older than me. As for alone, I could be. There have definitely been times in my life when I've been alone. It was certainly better than being in a bad relationship. Once you've accepted your fears, they no longer rule you.

A confident, happy person is aware of their surroundings. Their positive mood is contagious. Most of us have two types of friends. One type makes us feel happy and upbeat. We usually find ourselves laughing when we are around them. The other kind can be clingy and always wants to relate long-winded stories starring herself as the victim. The happy ones we long to see when we're apart. The second type you see coming and wonder how you can cut the conversation short. The big difference is the happy person focuses on the people around them while the victim-friend obsesses on her own issues. All people, men included, like people who are interested in them. Take the spotlight off yourself. Focus on others. See other people for who they are and not for what they can do for you.

Picture yourself in the grocery store when a man comes striding down the aisle with a mini-cart (a tell-tale sign of possible singlehood). The man has his shoulders back. He's smiling and looking up. He scans the shelves and the people. Your eyes meet, and you automatically smile (you can't help yourself). He may say something, and you find yourself answering. The encounter may last mere seconds, but suddenly you feel different, happier. His upbeat mood spilled over onto you. He focused on you. Now do you see why confidence is so attractive?

Today, practice smiling at people. You'll have no clue how many people's days you'll brighten with just your smile. It is the first step in your self-confidence journey. Often we pay attention to our outward appearance and not enough to our inner self. Surprisingly, I've had great encounters with mud on my jeans and a ball cap hiding my hair because I focused on the other person.

Believe in yourself right now. You are okay today. I always thought when I lost a few pounds I might be sexy so I started belly dancing. I discovered women of all sizes wowing the audience with their sexy mood and attitude. In performance, we're taught to own the room. We act like we're IT. Surprisingly, the audience reflects back our attitude. If we put ourselves down, we'll find people who will treat us the same way. If we believe we are truly great people and well worth knowing, then we'll attract the same.

The first step to being irresistible is to believe it yourself. Right now, look in the mirror and tell yourself you're fine. I know it sounds silly, but we spend so much time doing negative talk—why not confident talk? When you act like you're wonderful, it transforms you into a person people want to be around.

Sure, you'll meet creeps, jerks, users, but as a confident woman or man (who knows their worth) you can kick them to the curb and go on. Of course, they're attracted to you. Who wouldn't be? You, my friend, are fine.

Date Like a Man

IN THE BEGINNING, WHEN I decided to date again, I got grief from my family. How many times did I want to marry? How many failed relationships did I want, and why did I want to date men? One of my sisters even questioned if our father hadn't spent enough time with me and that's why I wanted male companionship.

My initial answer was that I was heterosexual. That's why I wanted to date men. Still, many heterosexual women don't date. The most common refrain heard from women is they never dated after their divorce. Something went so terribly wrong they did not want to suffer through that pain again. I agree to an extent. On the other hand, am I depriving myself of a good relationship? The question is how to get there.

I needed help, so instead of paying ninety dollars an hour for a dating coach, I read their books. I gathered *Why Men Love Bitches* by Sherry Argov (2002), *Date Like a Man* by Myreah Moore and Jodi Gould (2001), and *Make Every Man Want You* by Marie Forleo (2008.) While all three books approached the dating topic differently, they had common themes and often agreed with each other. The first thing you need is confidence.

As women, we often are amazed that the short, chubby guy at a party will continue to hit on all the most beautiful women until he gets one who pays attention to him. His behavior exemplifies confidence. He feels like he is the prize each woman would be lucky to get. If a woman rejects him, that's her loss. He doesn't spend two weeks talking about what's wrong with him to his guy friends. Women tend to be more critical regarding their own appeal. We also invent whole laundry lists of why someone might not be interested in us based on OUR perception.

We spend our time detailing what is wrong with ourselves instead of celebrating who we are right now. In belly dancing, the familiar axiom is to act like we know what we are doing even if we miss a step. People respond to our confidence, even if it isn't real. Eventually, we will be the fabulous dancer we pretend to be. In the meantime, just have fun. The same applies to dating. Act like every man should want to know you. Amazingly, the men will come. Better yet, you'll attract more of the type of men you want to attract.

Before, when talking to a man, I'd spend a great deal of time apologizing or putting myself down. I ridiculed everything from my job to my past dating history because I didn't see myself as a catch. The result was I ended up with men who also put me down. If I don't see myself as wonderful, why should anyone else? A man I recently dated commented that I was an interesting person. I fought the urge to say how boring I really was. Instead, I agreed with him, and he immediately straightened up and leaned closer. My confidence drew him in where my regular self-deprecation would have pushed him away.

Find out what's great about you. Ask your friends. Go out on a voyage of self-discovery. Once you can name five things that make you unique and marvelous, you are on your way. Be the person you want to be and have the internal characteristics you want in a man. If you desire a financially secure and confident individual, then be that person. Opposites may initially attract, but they usually break up later. That brings me to a big difference between men and women who date, the mission statement.

At your business, there is always a mission statement on the wall. It is the reason you do what you do, or at least the initial cause. Most women date to find a significant other while men date for fun. That's why many women pursue dating with the same diligence they attack Black Friday shopping. It isn't about having fun; it's about landing the right guy. It is no wonder that after bagging the wrong man a woman doesn't want to go out in the field again. All that work for nothing. Men, on the other hand, want to have fun. That shouldn't surprise any of you. Women complain bitterly about a female who might date several men at once because she's acting like a man. Why not date for pleasure?

If you're reading my blog, then you've probably been in a relationship or marriage. You don't need a husband; instead, you need a man to find you fascinating and who longs to pamper you. We approach every relationship as if marriage is the end goal. By doing this, we chase away men who would be fun dates, or ones who could have been very nice short-term relationships. Most of us have tried the other route before; like deer hunters, we targeted our prospect and lured him closer before pulling the trigger. We find, often years later, that we didn't get what we thought we wanted. Think of dating as a discovery time. Men do, that's why they go out with several women, trying to decide what they want or what works. Then there's the fun factor.

The only way you are going to find someone you really like is by meeting lots of datable men. All those movies and books about bumping into that special someone when you first decide to date are fiction. Sorry, ladies, I wanted to believe in them, too. Maybe you know someone who met a great guy right out of the gate. I also know someone who won the lottery, but it doesn't mean it is going to happen to me.

Remember the short, chubby guy at the party? He had confidence. When he heard about the party, he immediately thought about all the women who would be there. He didn't think about the fact he didn't have a date. Secondly, he worked the numbers game. He didn't go to the corner to assume the fetal position when the first woman rebuffed him. Thirdly, he knew what he wanted and went after it. Do you know what you want?

The Numbers Game:
Dating Multiple Men

FOR THOSE WHO JUST DROPPED into the blog, I am detailing how to date like a man. Men seem to enjoy dating so much more than women. Ever wonder why? They approach it differently. A guy might think he gets to go to dinner with an attractive lady. He gets food, good conversation, maybe some wine and some entertaining thoughts about getting closer to the woman.

The woman, on the other hand, might decide ten minutes into the date that he's not the one. Maybe he did something that reminded her of her old boyfriend. He could have said something about the Colts' last game, and her old beau was a Colts fan, which means he's a loser. The next ninety minutes are pure misery as she answers her date's questions. The following day she whines to her girlfriends that she shaved her legs for that! There can be a reversal of the scenario too, but in the end, it's a numbers game. Men know this.

If you aren't out there meeting people how can you expect to meet prospective dates? If you don't go out a great deal, then how will you know if a man is right for you? Too many of us followed the Victorian period concept that there is only one perfect man or woman for us. Sometimes we moan and groan he got away. Well, that could be the end of it. I'll never meet anyone like that again. The truth is, I won't because everyone is different. I used to joke that I wanted to date the male equivalent of myself, so I did that once. It wasn't as great as I thought it would be, but I would never have known unless I got out there and played the dating numbers game.

Ladies, if you're open to it, date as many men as possible. Every day is full of opportunities if you want it to be. There are men who would like to go out with you, but you have to meet them, first.

The only man who comes to my house and rings the doorbell is the UPS man, and lately it's been the UPS woman. Decide first if you're open to it. I entertained myself in the summer by watching a television show called **Plain Jane**. The reality-based show focuses on a shy woman who is transformed into a confident flirt to pursue her secret crush. Often her crush did not return her interest, but she learned something important: how to talk to men in every-day situations. I watched shy women's flirting efforts with great curiosity. This was something I never did before...talk to random men. The woman had to signal she was open to flirting.

She did this by being aware of her surroundings. Her head was up, shoulders back as she strode with a confident gait, and she occasionally smiled, signaling approachability. If an attractive man made eye contact, she held it showing she was open to flirting. If the guy didn't say something first, she did. Casual inquiries allowed her to discover if a man was married, in a relationship, gay, or interested. Men familiar with the drill will volunteer information in the first sentence about their relationship state as not to prolong the encounter.

How many men do we pass every day that might be exactly what we are looking for? Most of you are snickering about this because it was television. This doesn't happen in real life. It has happened to me, but not until I was ap-proachable did I receive it.

I used to like to go to the grocery on Thursday because of the new sales promo, but the chatty men shopped that day too. Little did I know when they were asking me what cheese went well with what wine it was to strike up a conversation. It didn't hit me until my friend Charmaine mentioned she always asked attractive men their opinion on wine after checking out their left hand first. My handsome son complained that older women were always asking his opinion on wine in the grocery. The mating game was going on in the grocery, only I wasn't a part of it.

You can't work the numbers game if you don't meet people. Many times, we close down men's advances because we decide immediately they aren't our type. My sister cracks me up because she seems to think I should only date men that I would look good within the context of a magazine fashion spread. Someone about my build and coloring, maybe a little taller than me, if such a man existed, I think I would call him brother.

My daughter believes I should date reasonably fit men since exercise is so important to me. She may have a point because it is much easier to find a healthy male than fashion accessory material. Probably one of the most engaging men I've met is far from a fashion model, but he has charm. I would have missed him if I held on to the outdated version of what my type is. Meeting men, allows me to explore what my kind might be currently.

Be open to seeing a variety of people. You'll discover someone you may have overlooked before. When you make yourself approachable, please note I mean well-groomed and friendly, not slutty. You'll be amazed at how many men you will meet. Most of them are just looking for an opening.

The other day I met a gentleman while waiting in line at the post office on my lunch hour. When I walked up behind him, he turned and looked as people do whenever anyone enters their personal bubble. His eyes lit up, and he smiled, signaling he was friendly and open. Flustered, I looked away from the immediate invitation. The line was long so I decided to talk to him. He lingered at the door after his transaction, waiting for me to finish mine. No such luck. I had to repackage my priority mail Christmas box. An opportunity lost, but there will be more if I am open to them.

It is amazing that there are so many single people in the world when people despair of meeting anyone. We women talk about wanting alpha men, but we rebuff their attempts at pursuing without even knowing it. Do you think the guy in the grocery really wanted my opinion on what dog biscuit would be best for his dog? What am I, a dog food expert? If I were with it, I would have known three things about him: he's single, he's interested, and he's a dog person. So far, so good; instead I showed him my dog's preferred treat and headed off to the frozen food section.

There's another thing I forgot to mention about the numbers games: rejection doesn't hurt as much. I've been rejected a dozen times for different reasons, but I can't even remember the guys' names. This is from a person who sees familiar faces, but can't recall many names. Keep in mind, there are men out there who will be attracted to you. It's because you're a confident, approachable woman. Who wouldn't want to be near you?

Update: *Dating more than one man made me infinitely more* desirable, but it also helped me to slow down relationships and have a chance to evaluate them better. My failure to behave as if I was part of a couple actually relaxed the man. If a man didn't work out, then I didn't feel like I wasted weeks or months because I happened to be seeing someone else who did have potential.

Chemistry: The Science of Attraction

DO YOU BELIEVE IN LOVE at first sight? Books, songs, poems, even movies are based on this theory. Does it actually happen? If so, does it equate to a lasting relationship? Sometimes, we talk about having chemistry or sparks. If you don't have it at first, can it develop?

One of the online dating sites, you're able to tell why you refused a match. A member closed my profile before I even had a chance to send him an icebreaker. His reason was no chemistry. How could there be no chemistry when we never even met in person? He never read one of my witty emails. What probably happened is he looked at my photo and thought I wasn't a leggy blonde.

Some of us have an image of an acceptable date/mate hard wired into our system and will not even look at someone different. When dealing with chemistry, the first thing we notice is visual. Why do you think guys resort to flashy sports cars? Yes, some women will react to what a man drives. Therefore, even though I am amused that some men post profile pictures posing with their BMW convertible, speedboat, and airplane, it still snags those women who love the toys. These relationships based on stuff are very short lived. Call it possession chemistry. What about physical chemistry?

When a male and female are on the hunt, so to speak, they give off pheromones that let the surrounding public know they are open to advances. Ironically, we douse ourselves in cologne, but that isn't the smell that matters. While the guy is trying to chat you up, he is attempting to get closer. If you're interested, you allow him to move in closer, cutting out the other men for a moment. This allows both of you a chance to see if there are any sparks. We think we measure humor, charm, or intelligence. What we're really doing is reacting to his pheromones.

Countless women have related tales of dating wonderful guys who had everything going for them, but when they bumped into the ONE, they dropped Mr. Wonderful like a hot potato. It puzzles the rest of us who were rooting for Mr. Wonderful. What happened is that they met someone they reacted to more powerfully. Has this ever happened to you? Dating a perfectly acceptable man, maybe even engaged, when someone new roars on the scene and sweeps you off your feet. In the beginning, it is all about smell. Your primitive response is based on if he smells right to you. This happens on such a subconscious level we're barely aware of it. Women are more open to men while they're ovulating, which means men have a smaller window of opportunity than they realized.

The next step in chemistry is the kiss. This can make or break the attraction. One study I read was that American men don't even like to kiss, which is a bad deal for hooking a desirable mate because most women love to kiss. A smart man knows he can work himself out of trouble with kissing if he can get close enough. A man is able to excite a woman by exchanging his testosterone-laden saliva with hers (i.e. French Kissing.) Suddenly, a woman can be more intrigued by a person than she initially thought. She might be telling herself he isn't a good bet when he starts kissing her, but she soon forgets why he's a bad bet.

If things get hot and clothes start flying, a woman can find herself more attracted to a man after sex because of the release of Oxytocin into the female bloodstream. Oxytocin, surprisingly, is nicknamed the cuddle hormone. Women like to cuddle after sex because they feel all loving and warm due to the Oxytocin rushing through their system. This hormone causes you to bond to the guy even if he's a bad bet. The male doesn't have an immediate Oxytocin reaction so he may slip away. This is also the reason why some women continue to pursue bad boys. How do you avoid this awkward scenario? Simple really, don't jump in bed with a guy just because he makes your hormones fire. Get to know him first, and that takes time.

So yes, you can fall for a man on first sight, but it is lust, not love. He may fulfill the image you have of a desired date. Your pheromones are mingling well. The man is funny and charming. (Funny goes a long way with women. I will always give a man a second look and a second chance if he can make me laugh. I've also broken off relationships with men who seemed to have no sense of humor.) However, does this immediate chemistry equate a long-term relationship?

The answer is yes and no. Think for a moment. Have you ever been in a relationship that was purely physical? The physicality was great, but the relationship burned out fast because that was all there was. Too often, you see committed men and women drop out of a relationship to chase after a younger, hotter model. The result is usually the new relationship dies out quickly because it was purely physical.

On the other hand, many women and men reject potential dates because there is no chemistry. What is the happy medium? Chemistry can grow and develop as you get to know a person. This explains friends or co-workers who work side by side for years until friendship turned into love. Unfortunately, some women will reject a man who doesn't meet their height or occupation requirements before they even get to know him, so there is never any chance of chemistry developing.

I've met guys who, on first glance, weren't that attractive to me because they didn't match up to my type template. To give the persistent men credit, they still tried using humor. When I did look again, I saw something different. Men I would have initially rejected began to grow on me. How I looked at them changed, too. Suddenly, they were much more handsome than before because I actually knew more about them and I liked what I knew.

Chemistry can be a significant contibutor in the relation-ship. It is the thing that keeps you dating when you're unsure of the guy. Long distance relationships have to have chemistry to succeed. His kiss has to be amazing to travel hundreds of miles for one. There are plenty of men nearby who would volunteer for the job. The goodnight kiss usually seals the deal for the next possible date so it is crucial. The smart man sometimes leaves without a kiss just to leave the woman wondering.

In the end, does chemistry matter? Yes, it does. Most men would never date a woman they could not see themselves sleeping with. Does chemistry guarantee a successful relationship? No. There needs to be other foundations to build on besides how well you shake the headboard. Can chemistry develop? Yes and no. You may meet a guy who has all the characteristics of Mr. Wonderful, but you may never fall for him. On the other hand, you may meet someone and gradually get to know him over time and fall for him.

It is a wonderful feeling to look across the room, see your man and have your heart race after you've been together for a long time. Personally, I'm looking forward to this.

Update: *I recently heard a woman state you could have chemistry with a serial killer and not live to talk about it. That is true to an extent. I believe chemistry is more than hormones. It changes, too. The more in love you fall, the stronger the attraction grows. There is always the opposite effect too, wondering how you were ever attracted to such a person.*

Dating is like Shopping IKEA Clearance

DATING IS LIKE SHOPPING THE clearance room. I love clearance places because so often I find treasures that other shoppers overlooked. An interesting picture or a fun pillow could hide behind an ugly couch in the clearance room. A funky, enamel necklace rests underneath a mess of tangled, eighty percent off jewelry in a pricey department store. A beautiful, red coat stands alone in the corner since it is out of season, ignored by most shoppers. An unknown woman said it (so I can't take credit for it), but dating is like the IKEA clearance room. She explained it by saying everything is marked AS IS. You can't ask if the pillow comes in a different color or if the coffee table is available in teak. What you see is what you get. So why do we think it would be different with dating?

Most men have a few scratches and dents on them from failed relationships. Seems silly to think we could buff them out with a can of paste wax. Still, we want the men we date to be different by fitting into some preconceived notion of what an ideal companion would be like. Most women create in their minds a male version of themselves. This person would understand us, we rationalize, when in truth he would be super critical just like us. Who needs that?

My stepfather likes to joke that women are always shopping for the perfect man and once they find him they set out on a campaign to change him. It always seems funny when he says it, but it is too often true.

I thought I knew what I wanted when I walked into the clearance room, but now I'm confused. You see there is not that perfect dream couch or guy I've been imagining. My attempt to explain it to the salesperson has her shaking her head, muttering something about being so out of style. How could I get what I wanted if I weren't specific? It seems like what I want no longer exists. Maybe I'm losing my present and future by constantly looking back to the past.

I could leave the clearance room in disgust, muttering about not finding anything good, but I don't. I figure what we need isn't always what we think we want. Rather like Charlotte in **Sex and the City,** who kept chasing after guys she felt were appropriate for her lifestyle and background only to fall for a short, bald Jew with a hairy back. I should worry that I get my gems of wisdom from a defunct television show.

Do I even need to be in the clearance room? Maybe I shouldn't be shopping…I mean dating. If I think of dating as being a big game hunter and I'm out to bag a man, maybe I should go home. Still I think of a chant from the book by Marie Farleo, **How to Make Every Man Want You**, *date for fun, not to find the one*. When I remember that, I can embrace dating again. It is fun to discover new people and trade quips over a glass of wine.

I think the whole story about the IKEA clearance room was to point out you have to accept people AS IS. Often people discard people who don't fit into the norm.

What if your soul mate is working right beside you? The funny guy you always have lunch with and remembers your birthday when your own mother forgets. Maybe you've dismissed him because you didn't consider him the right model for your lifestyle. People assess strangers in under ten seconds. Will they be a friend, an enemy, lover, or someone we walk by without acknowledging? Who wouldn't be mad knowing they had less than ten seconds to make a good impression. It is especially dangerous if you don't know the clock is running. It could be a moment you're off your game or a bad hair day. Unfair...so why do that to other people? Getting back to the clearance analogy, I often return to work with items I picked up at a deep discount.

My fellow workers are amazed that I bought something at a local store that they never saw. Since there is the only one decent store in town, everyone shops there. I picked up something that hundreds of other women ignored. The difference was I dug deep, unearthing my find.

Sometimes you have to dig for that particular fellow. Other times you have to do the prep work since he is afraid of approaching you. Yes, the non-players hang back certain of rejection. The hasty assumption is if they aren't taken then they're losers. Sometimes, people have the similar opinion about the clearance room. I often walk out with items that women are surprised were even in the room, but if you don't look, how will you know?

When you enter the clearance room, be it shoes or dating, keep an open mind. If you walk in with the idea you will only accept a six-foot tall physician, you will probably be walking out alone. It also reminds me of the Russian proverb, "Be careful what you wish for because you might get it." Getting what we want isn't always what is best for us.

Don't be afraid of the clearance room. Remember, we (women) are also in the clearance room.

Soulmates

WHO LOOKS FOR A SOULMATE? Anyone who reads astrological advice, takes magazine quizzes to measure their current or potential boyfriend for soulmate-ness, or even goes out on a date is looking for a soulmate. Most of us won't admit it for fear of ridicule. The idea of a soulmate is hard-wired into American culture. Most dating services use the premise of finding a soulmate, so it equates that people do want to find theirs.

The idea of a soulmate, surprisingly, comes most recently from the Victorian period. People frequently married for financial or practical reasons. The bride might marry to bring her family's standing up, either financially or socially. The concept of marrying for love wasn't popular until Queen Victoria married her beloved Albert. The idea shocked the public, but the adoration and support the staid Queen displayed for her husband excited general views on marriage. While Queen Victoria could never be compared to literary, lovelorn heroines, she openly referred to Albert as her soulmate. The real question is what is a soulmate?

The original Greek myth had the soulmate being a two-faced creature with four legs and arms plus a great deal of power. This being had two souls in one body. All emotional needs for love and devotion were met within the creature. There was no reason for it to look to the gods for guidance or worship. This angered the jealous gods who tore the creature asunder and threw the halves to separate ends of the earth. In the movie, **The Butcher's Wife**, Demi Moore's character explains this story. The creatures must spend the rest of their lives asking everyone if they were their soulmates, since once separated they could not recognize one another. Another version is that the creatures are dogs. That's why they are constantly sniffing each other's butts to see if the other dog is their soulmate. Supposedly, that was where they were connected, not the most romantic version. I am sure that isn't the version Queen Victoria was thinking of when she referred to Albert as her soulmate.

The dictionary defines soulmate as having a natural affinity for the other intellectually, physically, and sexually. Of course, there is a great love for each other across every area of the spectrum. According to online respondents, when posed with the question of the reality of soulmates, their answers differed. Some women believed a real soulmate ultimately knows what the other needs or is thinking without any words. This explains why women get miffed when their significant other doesn't have a clue what's wrong. Men aren't much better in their expectations. Often, they expect their soulmate to fulfill their fantasies without knowing exactly what they are. Expectations are high for a soulmate. The first requirement must be clairvoyance.

Can one person meet all your needs? Is there only one person who is your soulmate? The Victorian concept insisted there was just one. That has led many men and women to engage in a lifelong search for that one elusive person, sometimes rejecting people who might have enriched their lives. Often people will despair if they believe they have somehow missed their soulmate due to death, sickness, or location. The soulmate concept rationalizes bad behavior. A man or woman who walks out on their current family to chase after their alleged soulmate is only using it as a weak excuse. Finding your soulmate gets even trickier if you believe in reincarnation.

Can you ever actually find a soulmate? If you are looking for a psychic friend who can read your mind and is able to deliver on all your desires ASAP, then I hate to burst your bubble, but it won't happen. I do know couples that fit together very well, and I guess they would define my expectations of what a soulmate is since they respect, love, and support each other. The other major factor is they enjoy being with each other. Sure, they can function on their own, but together they are stronger. This goes back to the original soulmate creature who so angered the gods with its strength and love.

It brings to mind the concept of a good relationship that helps you be your best self. It is certainly better than the alternative. So how do you find this soulmate? If I knew, would I be writing this blog? I have some ideas, though. I think if you're open to all sorts of different people, you might run across those you could be compatible with. There will always be more than one. The big job now is deciding which reasonably like-minded person would be the best match. Someone you would want to wake up to every day. After all, that is one of the requirements of soulmates, to spend the rest of your lives together.

Update: *Yes, I do believe in soulmates, but they come in all shapes and forms. My soulmate and I are very similar in many ways. On the other hand, a good friend found her soulmate in a man who was almost her direct opposite in every way.*

The Dangerous Allure of the Bad Boy

WHY DO WE LOVE THEM?

Did you know American women have a strong preference for bad boys over any other culture? Why is that? American media glorifies the hot-looking, bad boy. Think of James Dean, James Bond, and other fictional bad boy types. As American women, we want it all. We want the hot guy who makes our hearts flutter and will also stick around and be a great dad. Not unlike the newly divorced, fifty-year-old man who wants a hot, twenty-year-old babe to have endless sex with, and who waxes his car while he naps. The truth is neither fantasy has a chance of happening.

Americans love Disneyworld because we like to believe dreams really do come true. That brings me back to the bad boy. He's eye candy. He definitely has the look, the swagger, and the sexuality. He enters the room on a testosterone driven wave. Females' heads swivel, their smiles grow wider and inviting. Men feel it too, but their instincts respond to a threat by becoming huffy or dismissive to the bad boy. This always makes them look petty. If they were more in touch with their primitive side, they'd immediately attack the bad boy and push him out the door.

Besides good looks, what does the bad boy have that the nice guy doesn't? He has attitude and plenty of it. He knows every woman in the room wants him. Talk about self-confidence! He has elevated cockiness to an art form. He doesn't need to be nice to women because they are responding to him on an instinctual level. A strong, alpha male enters the room and pheromones go on red alert, informing women that prime mating material is in the area. Years of watching movies where women fall at the feet of bad boys and reading endless romances, where the alpha male sweeps the woman off her feet, reinforce this belief. The sad fact is no matter how much women talk about wanting a kind, thoughtful man they will respond to a dominant, alpha male every time, even if it is for a short period. Women traditionally follow a strong, male lead.

Ironically, the bad boy doesn't get the girl by telling her she's beautiful. Instead, he gives her left-handed compliments like "you could be hot if you did something about your clothes." The woman immediately wants to know what she should do about her clothes because she wants to be hot for this man. The bad boy may hit on the girlfriend because women usually travel in pairs. In that case, the woman wants what she sees slipping away from her and tries even harder to catch the bad boy's eye. Do you know they even have classes for men on how to act like a bad boy?

The only problem is if you're an average guy and you try to act like a bad boy, you just come off sounding rude. The bad boy has charisma, humor, and loads of sex appeal. His words may be saying your dress is hideous, but his eyes are promising to peel that dress off your body. He also has pacing down to a science. He knows when to pull back to leave a woman intrigued. Always keep in mind a bad boy is a short-term venture. He knows he's not staying around. Too bad most women seem ignorant on this point. Instead, they believe if he meets the right woman everything will change.

Some women believe they can shape the bad boy into a

devoted family man. Remember the only person you can change is you. Bad boy is what he is. You respond to his undeniable charm. Maybe he's even yours for the night, but not for long. It isn't in his nature to be a one-woman man. He's gone before you ever really know anything about him. It is just as well; his irresponsible, bad boy ways would eventually grate.

In other cultures, women don't want bad boys because they want someone who is responsible. The dependable male with a steady job appeals to them. They know he'll be around to raise the children. Why are American women obsessed with bad boys? The fact that most American women are supporting themselves is one factor. They aren't necessarily considering bad boy for the breadwinner role. Instead, they see him as an avenue for the mythical, screaming, monkey sex they've heard so much about but never experienced. A brush with a bad boy allows a woman to walk on the wild side if only for thirty minutes. Another is the belief we can have it all.

Newsflash: You can't have it all. Choices have to be made. Most women who rode the roller coaster of having a relationship with a bad boy welcome the stability that comes with a nice man. Others become addicts and chase after bad boys despite friends' warnings. Now your suitable man might occasionally enjoy playing the bad boy role, but he'll still be around to take the kids to soccer practice. If he wants to don a leather jacket, mirrored sunglasses and straddle a Harley, make sure you jump on behind him. It could be a memorable ride. Maybe you can have it all.

Update: *The media perpetuates the myth that the right woman can tame and change the irresistible bad boy. This is a lie. He may want to change for a woman who doesn't swallow his bad boy act. In the end, it is all up to him.*

Pursued Vs. Pursuing

WHO REMEMBERS WOMEN'S LIB? I do. I may even have an ERA NOW button stored somewhere. Let's face it. Women are not operating the same playing field as men, paycheck or otherwise. The big question: Is it okay to be the pursuer in the dating game? This is a tricky question, and you have to define what pursuer means.

The fact that you made the decision to date means you are obviously going to put yourself out there to meet men. It's one thing to introduce yourself at a party and even make a coffee date as opposed to constantly emailing, calling, or texting a man, especially when he doesn't reciprocate. That not only looks needy, but it is also on the stalker-ish side.

You have friends who when they meet a guy will roll out the red carpet. On the premise, they've met Mr. Right, they make a five-course meal and serve it in a black, lace teddy on their second date. While the man may enjoy the pampering, he's gone within a month. What gives? Your friend wanted to show her potential man all she had to offer. It wasn't that what she had to offer wasn't good, just too much too fast. The man didn't appreciate it because he didn't work for it, anticipate it, or even have a chance to feel special. The lavish display gave the opposite message that this was something she did for almost every man who made it to date two.

We tend to respect what takes work and time. Children

who spend their own allowance money on a toy will treat it better than a gift. They remember how much work went into it. Men are like this. I got this fact from men! Sure, it is nice when a woman approaches them and makes the initial move, but a woman who always keeps making the moves leaves him with nothing else to do. When does the guy get to fulfill his traditional role as the pursuer?

Some shy guys need to be pursued, or else they'll never go out on a date. There is some truth to that. A woman who does ask the guy out should make sure it's her last obvious pursuing move because the next move is his. The flip side of this whole argument is the entirely passive guy. You know the one. In his effort to please, it is always "whatever you want, dear." Guys will sometimes complain that women don't appreciate good men anymore. It depends on what you define as good. A wimpy man who allows a woman to make all the decisions gets old fast, even for an opinionated person like me who likes to make decisions.

Men like what they don't have or what they think they might not get. They also like to think of themselves as the pursuers…even if you're allowing yourself to be pursued. There is nothing like a little doubt or insecurity to make a man pursue harder. I got a real life example in my own life due to the fact I don't listen to voice mail. If I see someone has called me, I'll call him back, but often I don't see that call. My family will keep calling until I do answer. A bad habit, but I doubt I'll break it. About once a week to ten days, I listen to all my voicemails. That's when I discovered one man had called me twice. I texted him with a general message and made no mention of his phone calls. His response was very enthusiastic.

He could have acted hurt or even refused to answer my

text, but he didn't. Instead, he put on his pursuer cap because I appeared elusive. If I mentioned my failure to listen to voicemail, I just sound irresponsible. Maybe he thinks I am so overwhelmed with men asking me out that I was only able to text because due to limited time. Mentioning my state of constant absent-mindedness would probably not endear me. Why do we want to share our flaws on the first date?

If a guy is around for the fourth or fifth date, then he is willing to deal with your shortcomings because he has a few of his own. If you want a man to pursue you, don't regale him with all the details of your previous relationship. Be mysterious. Don't tell everything. I used to think I had to mention all my failed relationships. Do you want to hear about all his failed relationships? Even if you think you do, you're only fooling yourself. No one wants that. If you insist on rehashing past loves it becomes a therapy session instead of a date. Is that what you want? Keep in mind, you want his attention on you, the pursued, not on the ones who got away.

Men like mysterious. I've heard it, even read it but didn't believe it. As a woman who talks too much, I thought it was my goal to reveal every tidbit of my life including my doubts about my ex's sexual orientation and a dislike for my ninth grade locker partner. This did not benefit me. It may have made some men run screaming into the night. It is rather freeing to realize my life does not have to be on an examination table. There are things I don't tell my family. Why would I want to tell a man I've known at best a couple of hours? Mysterious can be good. He pursues you to learn more. Keep in mind you never have to reveal all. Remember this if you befriend a potential beau on social media. One

younger man publicly bragged that going through a woman's social media saved him easily three to four dates. He
often decided against pursuing a woman due to her posts.

There is a standard joke among women my mother's age
that they allowed a man to chase them until they caught
him. They knew all along which man they had set their cap
for. Their girlfriends knew, too, and probably the guy as
well. Still, on his part, there was a bit of insecurity that she
could prefer another male or lose interest, so he needed to be
clear where his interest lie. He did this by bringing small
gifts and squiring his girl around. There's a good chance he
also warned off other men. It reminds me of a nature show
where the male animal puts on his mating display to attract
a female and chases off the competition. Ever wonder if the
female animals talked amongst themselves. Pointing out
which male, they liked already, but allowed the man to feel
like he was the pursuer?

Update: *I joked on a blog that I allowed my husband to catch me
while I had decided on him from the start. This amazed him
because he believed he was pursuing me. He had to an extent.
Rather like primitive men, he demonstrated why he was superior
to other men as far as a mate.*

The Scripted Phone Call

OKAY, LET'S ADMIT IT. Aren't all stages of dating awkward? Maybe after seeing each other for about six months it becomes less awkward. By that time, you decided, or he has decided, you don't suit. Then it is onto a different awkward stage. I'm going to start with the stilted phone call. I've gone over my online prospects, and we've emailed back and forth a few times, but now it is time to step up the game to the phone call level.

This is nerve wracking for me because I honestly feel like it is a game, and I was never good at sports. By myself, I would sink that basket almost every time. Well, maybe that was when I was by myself...in my imagination. Same with the phone call. I'm brilliant before I get on the phone. In reality, there will be anxiety-provoking silences, probably due to worrying that my voice is too low or raspy. Then there's my accent. Is it too late to develop a faux British accent? For all my worries, things often don't even progress to this stage.

Some men don't really want to date. They rather like the prospect of dating as opposed to the actual date. I had a yearlong email relationship only to have the man disappear from cyberspace after we arranged to meet. Of course, you're wondering why I continued to email for an entire year. He was sweet, and it was nice to get his upbeat messages. When I decided to push to meet, he seemed all for it. I used tickets to a comedy club as a lure, but about two weeks before the actual event he cut all contact. He did not respond to my emails. I couldn't bring myself to call. A woman needs some pride. A few of you are saying married. Perhaps, he just realized it.

Most men want to talk on the phone. They are going through their own checklist. No doubt, they peered at my tiny profile picture wondering how old it is and how much it has been enhanced. The next step is voices. A low, masculine timber does it for me. Still, there are so many pitfalls in the call. I can only list my own. All I do at work all day is talk and make up things as I go. It makes sense a phone call would be a no brainer, which translates to no brain function of any measurable type while using the phone.

The first phone call is a minefield; everything from not having a clue what to say to not being able to make decipherable sounds emerge from my throat. I called a gentleman that I was meeting and croaked hello. Maybe he thought it was a bad phone connection, but at least he didn't hang up. Then some men just don't talk, never mind croaking back. After keeping up both sides of the conversation and introducing topics, I'm whipped. Normally it isn't that difficult to have a conversation with myself, but with another person involved, it is exhausting. I may not make my decision to mark Mr. Incommunicado off the list, but the pencil is definitely in my hand. I am puzzled why a man with such a great picture seems to be lacking a personality. Don't answer this, I know.

Moving on to the next phone call. Usually, the men send me their numbers so I can call at my convenience. It is hard to catch me at home. Perhaps they might think I am screening my phone calls (which I am), but I will pick up if able.

That's why I like to call the first time.

Off to awkward conversations, which are information-gathering missions in disguise. The CIA could get hints from online daters. Is he going to say anything very weird that kills any interest? As a hard-core dog person, I find a man without a dog slightly suspicious. In truth, I guess I am looking for reasons to disqualify a guy. Why waste time with someone who would not be a good fit? The usual conversations center on work, children, and hobbies. I faked my way through entire sports conversations. Because I have sons and work with the football coach, I am able to fake sports.

Why do this? I don't know how to not do this. The man starts talking about what he knows, and I respond. There are the conversations where the man talks about his various exploits and I listen, another type of awkward conversation. There is the dreaded ex conversation where I feel a bit like a therapist. Then there is the conversation where everything clicks. My daughter strolls by several times and raises her eyebrows as I giggle. She mouths the words, "Geek Humor." How did she know we were talking about Star Trek? Then it happens.

He asks what I'm doing for the weekend. I managed to make it all the way to the date discussion. Now, I just have to make it to the meeting. I have high expectations, but also great anxiety.

Can you remember your most awkward conversation? A prospect wanted me to explain in detail why I was divorced and what I did to cause the divorce. My answer was I got married. As for my rude caller, I hung up on him.

Update: *I've discovered phone calls will not break a relationship. An awkward phone call does not signify a relationship will flop. Don't judge a person by their first conversation.*

Chasing Love

IT'S FRIDAY EVENING, and I am shoulder deep in a hot bath as Elton John sings about a candle in the wind. I know he is talking about Marilyn Monroe. The blonde beauty fascinated me as a teen, and I devoured as many biographies about the sex symbol as I could lay my hands on. One written by her housekeeper entitled **Marilyn Monroe: Confidential,** especially caught my attention because it explained her actions as an endless pursuit of love.

Marilyn dated and married famous men because she thought they would bring her that most desired gift: love. Most of her husbands and lovers viewed her more as an exotic flower they might collect. Her most well-known husband, Joe DiMaggio, was so intensely jealous of any man who even looked at Marilyn that he eventually drove her away. Her biography listed one heartache after another. The woman who epitomized beauty and physical love couldn't actually hold onto love. She commented to her housekeeper that men enjoyed her screen image, not who she was. All she really wanted was someone who could love her, Norma Jean…not Marilyn Monroe.

Marilyn's desire to be loved for who she really was could be any woman's plea. Love who I am; not who you think I am. Princess Diana, whom Elton John modified the candle song for experienced her own brush with elusive love. Diana actually married a prince, but they did not live happily ever after. Even though she professed to love her prince in the beginning, things didn't work out. The question was, did she fall for a princely image or did the prince propose to a woman he felt he could mold into his princess? Before she died, she stated she was in a love relationship, which shows even princesses are constantly looking for love, and like the rest of us, not always finding it immediately.

In fact, more than fifty percent of married or committed couples feel like they aren't in a love relationship. Divorce statistics prove that there are many differences of opinions of what constitutes love after the 'I do's.' The real question is what does love look like?

According to Dave Ramsey, the founder of **Financial Peace University**, financial stability expresses love to a woman. Women are nesters, and they appreciate the ability to keep the nest and occasionally re-feather it. Many men don't understand this since they are hunters. Instead of nesting, they travel, leave stable jobs, and drag the wife and children along on the next great adventure. These women may not feel the love because they are always working to keep their home base intact. It is understandable that women who constantly abandon friends and family may not feel like they've captured love since they're continually off balance.

However, many men do understand stability. These same men work hard and maintain the family home. They show their love with actions, and yet their wives may still leave, stating he wasn't loving or romantic enough. Their love language was different. He kept busy doing actions for his wife to say, "I love you" while she wanted long walks while holding hands. Author Gary Chapman explains the five types of love language in his book, **The Five Love Languages** and on his website of the same name. On the website, there is a quiz to discover your love language and the love language of your sweetie.

Your Past Can Destroy Your Future

HAVE YOU HAD SOME BAD DATES, failed relationships, and even disappointing marriages? Then you have a past, and it may be hurting your future prospects. It isn't entirely like my mother's chant about being a three-time loser because you failed before, but it does have a lot to do with the fact you failed. We take our histories of abusive spouses, conniving boyfriends, and stalker-ish acquaintances with us on every date. That's right. We carry the baggage in, and here are the results:

"All women use men," states my date. He lists in detail how women have used him. I know I'm not a user, but I can tell by his bitter attitude he already believes I am. I will only disappoint him somehow, so it isn't even worth trying to convince him otherwise. Women do this too and wonder why there is no second date.

The history buff—this man somehow relates everything he's done in his adult life back to a woman he dated or was in a relationship with. Simple questions about concerts he's been to or music he likes results in a recitation of concerts he's been to with other women in the exact same place you are sitting at the time. This pushes the ick factor to the nth degree. If a female did this, we would probably say she was insecure and trying to show her date she was loved before. When a guy does this, several times, it is thoughtless, and you do wonder what point he is trying to make. Hey, I dated people, but somehow I manage not to bring them into every conversation.

Your past can get in the way of your future if you let it, and plenty of people let it. Think of your worst fears. For some, it is the fear of a man leaving them because it has happened before. This concern is placed before the potential boyfriend like a golden fleece. If he fails to answer the leading questions appropriately, then he fails to earn the next date. Too bad, he didn't get a study guide.

Many times when we leave a bad relationship, we tend to think everything about the previous man as flawed, which isn't true. I refused to date men I thought looked like my ex-husband, and it even extended to his hobbies. Since he was an avid marathoner and bicyclist, just the mention of running had me jogging the opposite way. This sudden aversion to all things that had gone on before did not serve me well. I am an active person, and I was passing on active men, too afraid they would be like my ex-husband.

Sometimes instead of the bad boyfriend syndrome, you may be packing around the old flame memory. Your first serious boyfriend, the great one that got away, tends to hang in the back of your mind. He is more special because he was your first from slow dance to goodnight kiss. Your memories may not be entirely accurate. Time tends to let us don the rose-colored glasses. At the age of forty, more women are searching for old classmates in hopes of finding their long-lost love. Hearts are warmed by tales of young lovers separated and reunited again years later, but that isn't the usual ending. Women anxious to meet up with their high school sweetheart are often shocked when he's bald, over-weight, and not exactly charming. What happened to that dream man in their minds?

He was in their minds. All those wonderful qualities...he may not have ever had. This was brought home to me about my high school sweetheart who I thought was an excellent fellow. We dated on and off for seven years. Everyone thought we'd eventually marry. I urged him to move to another state to take advantage of graphic art opportunities...and then I never heard from him again, not even a letter, despite the fact I wrote. It made me rethink that the man I'd been using to measure other men against didn't really exist.

Often we can joke about being attracted to the wrong kind of men. If we can't figure out why we cozy up to mama's boys or tolerate a man who is a workaholic, then we are doomed to repeat our mistakes. There is nothing sadder than seeing a friend engaged in yet another abusive relationship. We have to do the work to get out of the cycle. Sometimes, the work can be done on your own with a couple of blunt friends and a journal, but other times a therapist is needed. Beware jumping into dating before you understand why you do what you do.

Then there is the self-fulfilling prophecy. If I don't say it, even think it, my mother will remind me of all the previous bad relationships I've endured. Her unsubtle message is you've screwed up before, so why even bother. Unfortunately, many women enter relationships with this type of pronouncement hanging over their heads. They assume future relationships will suffer a similar fate. The tension is palatable. Sometimes, they will sabotage the budding relationship just to get it over with before it hurts too much.

What you can do is start fresh. Don't compare your date to anyone in your past. Let him be himself. Do enjoy YOUR time together. Do not waste precious time by inserting talk about past relationships. Those relationships are over. If they were so good, you'd still be in them. Why allow them to screw up an opportunity for future happiness.

I guess it all comes down to checking your luggage at the door. Actually, leave it there. Don't go back for it. You don't need it to go forward in love. In fact, it may keep you from getting through the door in the first place.

Update: *I will admit I've caught myself more than once picking up old baggage. Often, checking your baggage is an everyday thing.*

When Dates Go Very Bad

WHAT DO YOU CONSIDER A bad date? Is it when a date shows up looking like the grandfather of the man pictured in the online profile? It could be when extra people come along, such as friends, children, or relatives to check you out. One dating column advised the women to take along friends to judge the fellow. Seriously?

Then there's the time when your date mistakes you for a lady of the evening, and you have to explain that a combo meal does not buy him any action. Maybe your salesman date is convinced a date is a perfect venue to sell you a pricey whole life policy. Bad dates, where you merely irritate or bore each other, aren't all that bad, just a time waster. What if your date goes really bad?

Most people have heard a news story where a woman disappears after meeting someone at a nightclub. That's the extreme downside. Sometimes, you have an ordinary guy who doesn't do it for you, who keeps calling, texting, or even showing up at your job. Other times your stalker might be his current girlfriend who has found your number in his phone. How can you avoid the twisted date syndrome?

Be very, very careful about the information you give out. Many people online will use a nickname or a middle name so they can't be Googled or looked up in the white pages. If you live near a big city, use that as a location, not your small town. Watch the photos you put up. Make sure there isn't any identifying information in the picture. Are you in front of your house? Maybe your work logo is right behind you, or you're at your favorite golf course. This information can be used to locate you. After one date, a male friend of mine refused to go out with an overly aggressive female. The woman called him demanding to know why he wouldn't give her another chance. Finally, she blocked the end of his road with her car and refused to let him leave for work. Even though he was a big man, he was terrified, unsure if the woman was armed. Because of his community position, the last thing he wanted was to be front-page news.

What could he have done differently? Many things. First, he gave out too much information. He gave out his phone number and his neighborhood. Many online daters start with an email address that does not have any combination of their name included in it. This way they can communicate back and forth with someone until comfortable. Never tell a new person where you work until you are on the fourth plus date. Do you really want a disgruntled individual sitting in the parking lot waiting for you?

Photos are not something you want your new date to have. I've gone on first dates where the man photographed me to put on his cell phone. At first, I thought it made sense. Then I heard about these initial photos being used in a variety of ways such as showing the ex he was dating, or grandma that he did have a girlfriend and wasn't gay. Your image can be photoshopped; your head put on a different body and uploaded to the Internet. I know that sounds paranoid with a capital P, but it does happen. Do you want someone to have your photo that you don't know all that well? Don't get me started on the females who think it is appropriate to send sexy photos to someone they just met.

Everyone at his work has a good laugh. Don't kid yourself that these pictures are private. The date may not be the problem, but his creepy co-worker might be.

Never, ever, allow a new guy to know where you live. He seems nice, but he could go ugly on you. Women tend to stalk more than males. Knowing where you live and work allows them to shadow you. Even casual comments that you bowl on Wednesdays may have your rejected date showing up for league night.

Be wary of first dates who want you to come to their house. That isn't right on some levels. One gentleman called ahead to let his blind date know he was on his way and was surprised to find her wearing a ratty bathrobe and no makeup. When he inquired if she needed more time, she flashed him. The guy took off before she offered any more freebies. Another unfortunate welcome came in the form of his date's children calling him "new daddy." Others met up with not so ex-boyfriends toting firearms. On the other side, be wary of a person that never allows you to come to their home. If you are seeing someone for more than THREE months and you've never been to his house, something isn't right. It could be anything from a wife, hoarding issues, or lives with parents.

A major mistake happens when alcohol is involved, including revealing too much information. Why people reveal secrets to someone they just met I have no clue, but many do. The initial dates are not a good time to confess felonious activities or secret fantasies. This is blackmail material and can keep you in a union.

Now most of you are probably scared to date, but it is like anything else: if you know the danger, you can avoid it. Before I went snorkeling, I had to watch a slide show about underwater dangers. I was terrified of stepping on fire coral or meeting up with an octopus…neither happened. Instead, I had a wonderful time snorkeling. Same with dating.

If you have doubts, don't go out. If your instincts are telling you that this is a bad bet…then it probably is. Primitive people survived by listening to their instincts. You would do well to listen to yours. Hold back your personal information and talk about general items on your first date. Do have a dummy email to collect all your inquiries. Google your date if you know his real name. (Be aware online info isn't always correct or current because I Googled myself and found I was living in Georgia married to my ex-father-in-law.) Always drive yourself and arrive separately. Often dating sites have a verification process that your date can use to show he is who he said he is. Take care, so you don't find yourself sneaking through the restaurant kitchen to get away later. If you need to sneak out through the kitchen, do it. Your safety comes first.

The Dating Games

WOMEN TAKE THE MAJORITY OF the blame for playing games. I see many male, online profiles that claim they don't want women who play games. I am always puzzled what games they are talking about. I have a feeling it isn't Monopoly or Scrabble. What I really want to know is which games do men dislike so much? So I asked, reasonably discreetly. Some of you can imagine what an uncomfortable date I must have been. Still, men were willingly to discuss the matter.

A wealth of information came from asking about bad first dates, dates, and relationships in general. A guy can figure out his date isn't interested in him, but more interested in being seen on a date when her head keeps swiveling. The kicker is when an enraged boyfriend or husband shows up to threaten bodily harm. The man figures he gets off easy if the angry boyfriend just drags the game-playing woman home. This is the jealousy game, and any sucker will do. Don't make the mistake thinking that guys don't indulge in this game, too. They do.

If your new honey keeps taking you to out of the way places or insists he doesn't like to date in the city because of too many work-related acquaintances, then he could be a cheater! He may be cheating on a wife, or a girlfriend, or both.

The next game is a variation on a common theme of buying affection. The date might suggest pricey restaurants or theater shows she might want to see. If a man didn't spend enough money on a date, the woman might act miffed or even complain about it. This date would be offended if her date used a gift certificate to pay. After all, how can she measure her date's financial output if he cheats and uses a gift certificate? If the relationship progresses, the woman will suggest expensive gifts or trips she'd like. This same woman would have no problem refusing to see a man who didn't throw around enough money to suit her.

A former co-worker plays a condensed version of this game. She calls it "I want to go out to eat, and I'm too poor." As a beautiful woman, she has several men chasing her. She calls one and suggests she'd like to go out tonight. The excited man willingly agrees. The problem with this (she explains to me) is the man thinks it is a date since he pays. When I point out it is a date, she jokes she would never consider him as boyfriend material in a million years, but he will serve as a meal ticket. She makes sure not to call the same guy for a couple of weeks so he won't assume they're dating. I'm willing to bet good money that he thinks they are.

A common game women play is sex for love. The woman who offers sex early on usually has the opportunity of watching a man walk out of the door or suggesting the position of a friend with benefits. Sometimes the women will assume the position of a friend with benefits without even realizing it. Men will usually take what the woman is offering, but do not feel the same bond as the female. In fact, many men will resent women who try to manipulate them with sex…even though it does take two to tango. Unfortunately, this type of game playing doesn't result in an exclusive relationship. It is a hookup.

A variation on the sex for love game is when the woman is constantly promising sex by word, actions, and clothing but never delivers. She sends mixed messages and strings a man along with the possibility of having sex. It is a possibility that never materializes. This aggravates the average male, but it usually takes him at least seven-plus dates to figure out he's being played. He often excuses his date's hands off policy to being old fashioned until he finds out she wasn't so standoffish with other men. A played man may be suspicious of all women for a while.

The filler date is one most of us are guilty of playing. This is someone you date until someone better comes along. The filler date is forgotten when a more promising prospect comes along. The hopeful person stays at home waiting for a call from her beloved. Clearer communication could have avoided this scenario. If a man or woman wants to play the field, then he or she should be honest about it. This allows the other person to know where he or she stands.

The soft landing game often occurs when a woman is between relationships. She picks an accommodating man who for some bizarre reason wants to fulfill her every wish. He mistakenly thinks he has a prize. While he meets her financial and physical needs, she decides what her next step will be...and it definitely won't be with him. Often, these women will move in with the man creating the illusion that there is a relationship. Once she moves in, she isn't as loving as she used to be since she now has what she wanted, a soft landing spot between relationships. Women who are not in the habit of standing on their own feet, but drift through life using men, usually play this game.

A variation of this game involves unemployed or underemployed men moving in with a woman they hardly know.

Often the woman makes the mistake of suggesting it after listening to his tale of woe. Even ex-husbands have played this card. It is hard to move on when your current mistake is sleeping in the living room.

Then there is the drama queen. Most of us went to high school with her. Everything has to be about her all the time, 24/7. The queen is high maintenance with a capital M. This woman appears to be more sophisticated and colorful than ordinary women. The attention must always be on her, thus the drama. Often, she'll pick public fights to draw attention to herself. In turn, she'll be rude to service people for the same reason. She believes the world revolves around her. She is often in a snit when others don't realize this. The queen never thinks of her man because all her time and energy is on her. She may also have children, and this is where the soft landing guy comes in big time. He gets to take care of the children. She'll use her children to get what she wants while the man thinks he is helping the kids. Intelligent men drop her immediately, but less secure men hang on until they are old news.

It is no wonder men specify they don't want women who play games. When you're in a relationship, you don't recognize the games until you're just about ready to exit, or have exited, the relationship. Occasionally, you have friends who insist you're an enabler, but you manage to rationalize why you aren't. As for the game players, a man stating he doesn't want to play games doesn't scare them off. Instead, the man that inadvertently reveals he's been in a game before will end up in the game again. It is the equivalent of waving a steak in front of a dog.

One dating book I read revealed when we show our fears to a potential date or even relationship wounds, we endanger ourselves. A man who confesses several women have used him financially signals to his date that she can shake him down for money. A woman who complains that her last two boyfriends cheated on her suggests she will tolerate cheating. (This is one reason not to share past relationships info early on if at all.) We all like to think a decent person wouldn't treat us like that, but often you never know if your date is an honest person or not. In the beginning, they are who you think they are...and sometimes they are a game player even if you don't think they are. Good game players never show their hand.

Keep in mind, men expect you to be a game player even when you aren't. Innocent remarks often sound gamey when they aren't. Be clear; explain if you think he's unsure. You would appreciate it if he did the same for you. Men can be guilty of playing the same games as women.

Update: It is obvious I received most of my games from men who'd been played. The games played by men, in my experience, were where you tended to take on a combination role of secretary and mother; handling everything from cooking dinner to social engagements. Many women would think this is being traditional. It's not. My deceased aunt who passed in her late eighties expected her husband to help with the housework, child rearing, even cooking. There's nothing traditional about being used.

Another game is a bit of the friend with benefits game where you never seem to do anything interesting or go anywhere nice. The man is saving his best efforts for someone he believes is worthy while you manage on pizzas and video rentals.

Then, there is the vanishing boyfriend who is afraid of commitment; he tends to disappear after three dates. He returns in a couple of months with excuses. Don't buy into them. Either he's allergic to relationships or another woman caught his eye when he left you high and dry.

Dating Red Flags

I READ AN ARTICLE ABOUT a woman who tried every dating book, online dating, and even a professional matchmaker. I never gleaned from the short article if she ever found that special someone, but I did notice two red flags. Red flags are warning signs to discontinue the date or sneak out the back way if possible. Her first warning flag was she talked about all she wanted a man to do for her. This included buying her the new car she couldn't afford. She also wanted someone drool-worthy to parade in front of her friends. Those are rather noticeable flags, but some are more subtle.

A man who is unhappy with his job is a bad dating prospect. Men's jobs define who they are. If he is unhappy at work, he won't be happy anywhere. Dating this unhappy camper will end up with you both being unhappy. Do you really want to listen to a litany of work-related complaints?

The flip side for men is avoiding women who are unhappy with their weight. There is a real difference between wanting to drop five pounds and despising your shape. Women identify themselves with their weight. They also value themselves by how they FEEL about their looks. If a woman is down on herself, then it is hard to be up on someone else. A heavy-set woman can have a healthy self-image while an average-sized woman may dwell on weight concerns.

Another red flag is the straight out of a relationship guy

or gal. I am amazed to see men who are just starting the divorce process (so they say) by online trolling for a date. Anyone who has been divorced or newly single for less than a year is very fragile. They need a relationship to prove they are still desirable. What you get is an emotionally needy person who has yet to find his own feet and will lean on you heavily. Caution: after you helped him on his feet, shored up his confidence and held his hand, he will drop you for a less helpful woman. The twist with the newly divorced woman is sometimes she needs the financial support the man provides.

Then there is the relationship king or queen. This person seems to have never been without a date or a significant other for his entire adult life. This should be very scary to a potential date. Why can't he spend time alone? Why does he need someone by his side 24/7? Sometimes to justify our choice we tell ourselves he is such a good prospect, that naturally other women want him. What other women want him? Desperate, needy women, that's who.

In the movie, **Ten Ways to Lose a Guy**, the main character gets bad dating advice from her assistant who chases off every man she's ever dated. One way the assistant did this was to imagine each man was her future husband. By the end of the date, she had names for their children. The male version of this might even want the waiter to take a picture of the two of you for your future grandchildren. This man assumes a great deal before you've even ordered dessert. Despite his confident front, this man is desperate. It is okay to cut the date short to visit a sick friend.

The dictator roars in on a date and demands to have everything his way. He terrorizes waiters and valets alike. He thinks he impresses everyone with his importance, but he just comes off obnoxious. Keep in mind that no one is good looking or rich enough for you to put up with this type of nonsense. Some of you will have to find this out on your own.

The time-challenged date arrives very late with no excuse. At first, you figure it was a one-time thing until you see a pattern emerge of lateness, missed or canceled dates. By accepting the first dubious behavior, you've set yourself up for continued disrespect. At college, when a professor didn't show, you waited fifteen minutes and left. It seems fair to give a date the same treatment.

The flirt is usually a good-looking charmer who feels the need to impress every woman within five hundred feet. He flirts lavishly with the restaurant hostess until you wondered which one of you is on the date. He compliments random women as if he dispensing grace. He tries to catch women's eyes and smiles at them. He is under the impression that all women want him. Aren't you the lucky one because you have him for the night?

Another warning sign is when someone you just met wants you to do outrageous things. On your first or second date, he asks if you'll drive him to the airport to make a four a.m. flight. If he asks you to pick up his dry-cleaning or boots he just ordered, don't, you're not his errand boy. Extract yourself from his clutches the first time he asks you to pay the bill because he forgot his wallet. How often have you walked into a restaurant and forgot your purse?

The randy, octopus guy describes a man most women have dated at least once. He uses every opportunity from opening the door to helping you on with your coat to cop a feel. At dinner, he slips off his shoes, and his feet go wandering along with his hands. Forget slapping his hands away, he only sees it as a game. This date is your reason for arriving in separate cars.

Sometimes the guy is excellent. The date is going well. It is obvious he's both intelligent and charming. Besides being good-looking, he's also financially stable. It's great he isn't bitter like so many of the men you've met before. You know he's a great guy because he speaks so well of his ex. They have an excellent relationship he coos. They even go on vacation together. Did you miss something here?

The opposite of 'I love my ex' date is all women are scum date. Of course, you wouldn't have gone out with him if you knew this. He reveals this by mentioning how his no good, cheating girlfriend left him for his best friend or his ex took him to the cleaners. It may all be true, but the first date is not the place for these types of disclosures. He is eager to let you know how the female gender left heel prints on his heart. He also stereotypes by saying things like all women lie. Do you really want to be stereotyped?

Every male red flag has a female equivalent. Some red flag dates are women only. The gold digger date is a woman who measures the value of her escort on how much he spends on her. She's going for as much as she can get and may not care if she sees the man again. One man told me his date was highly offended when he used a gift certificate to pay for their pricey dinner. She seemed to think the gift certificate invalidated the date. She told him he should put away the certificate and pay cash if he wanted the date to count. I am sure those two never went out again, but she went on to relay to her friends how much her date cost...not mentioning the gift certificate, I'm sure.

Update: *Any man or woman who spends a good deal talking about another person they dated isn't a good bet. What they are really saying is they wished you were that person.*

Dating and the Fear Factor

FEAR IS OUR BIGGEST OBSTACLE from having the life we want. It always has been and continues to be so. Think back to when your children were young or even when you were a kid. Can you remember how fearless you were? Do you remember when you stopped being fearless? Do you remember what you wanted to be? I wanted to be Superman. I jumped out the window of my second-floor bedroom and flew straight down to the ground. I made a few other attempts at flying and did not even get a scratch for my efforts. I stopped trying to fly, not because I actually got hurt, but because of the fear that I might get hurt, which my mother reinforced. Fear we might get hurt holds us back more than actually getting hurt.

When I was little, I fell off horses about fifty percent of the time when I attempted to ride. Most of our horses were green broke and didn't want to be rode. Bucked off might be a more appropriate description. My father made me get back on the horse every time, immediately. I couldn't stop and lick my wounds. I climbed back onto the horse each time. To this day, I am not fearful of riding a horse. Millions of people who have never ridden a horse or fallen off one, and yet they are afraid of the riding experience. So much so that they will not even get near a horse. Their fear is imaginary, but that doesn't make it feel any less real. Often, we rehearse our fear making it stronger. Who wants to do what they fear?

Almost thirty-four weeks ago, I decided to date intelligently and blogged about it. Was I frightened? It was incredibly scary (both the dating and blogging) and turns out, I had a good reason for my trepidation. I am twice divorced and have a handful of failed relationships that justified my fear. First, dating intelligently sounds like an oxymoron. The decision to use my academic background to research dating seemed odd at best, but I did learn—a great deal. Sometimes, I wish I could have learned it sooner.

My first shock came when married female "friends" attacked me for going public about dating. They ridiculed me behind my back and to my face, often doubting I had even gone out on the dates. They emailed each other about each blog, knowing I was on the same email loop. I had plenty of fears starting out, but this was never one. I figured my conservative mother would go ballistic whenever she got a whiff of the fact that I was putting such personal things online for the public to read. It just wouldn't be seemly…whatever that means.

Every time I took a chance and met someone new, I was petrified that this total stranger would find me lacking somehow. (This is the place where most women find themselves. This is the reason they don't date because of the fear of the unacceptable label.) Through dating, I discovered facets of myself I didn't know existed. Suddenly, I saw myself through others' eyes and found out I was both fascinating and mysterious. The same anxiety about being unattractive or boring was in almost every man I ever went out with, except for the few who knew they were perfect. I just didn't have the good sense to appreciate their perfection.

Dating is hard, especially the first date. You have two individuals who often are so anxious their words don't even make sense when they try to hold an ordinary conversation. Sometimes, they end up confessing they're bad with women or haven't been out in years. The worst first date conversational tidbit a man dropped on me was that his ex-wife left him for another woman. I'm not even sure why he told me that; perhaps he figured it would come up sometime and wanted to get it out of the way. Maybe he feared I would find out later and stop seeing him. I never saw him again so I have to wonder if it wasn't a legitimate fear. Most of our fears have no actual basis.

A book I started reading recently called **Life Unlocked** by Srinivasan S. Pillay, MD, explains how most of our motivations are from fear. We often think we act intelligently, but usually we respond out of fear. We rationalize our fears to make them sound like the right thing to do. A few of us have failed marriages to our names and can now see we married because we were afraid of being alone. Simply put we acted out of fear, not because of some grand passion. Once trapped in a bad marriage, many do not leave because of the same fear of being alone.

Dr. Pillay explains in his book that often we fear change and being wildly successful because we wouldn't know how to act. It would upset the world we know. We hear stories all the time to confirm our belief that being fortunate or lucky is not a good thing. People who win lotteries are often broke in less than two years because they attempt to live like millionaires on crack. Sometimes we are accustomed to our fear and a not so fantastic life. We never hear about people who wisely managed their winnings. No one is interested in those types of stories because they don't confirm our fears, but they still happen.

I remember two things my grandmother told me about

working with fear. Imagine the worst thing that could happen and develop a plan to deal with it. The thing never happened after I developed a plan to deal with it. The second thing she told me was to do the thing I feared. As the youngest child of the youngest child, I was seldom alone and babied as the last grandchild. The thing I feared the most was being on my own. I approached that fear at the grand age of twenty-four when I inadvertently traveled through Europe alone. My companion and I disagreed, and suddenly I was alone with five more weeks to fill. Each day, I would decide which country I was going to, where I would stay, where I would eat. In doing this I had many adventures, some downright scary, but I survived. I faced my fears and came back home a stronger person.

Facing your fears is the way to go. Know them. Is there a reason for them? Defuse them as if they were a bomb. Make a plan for handling them. Finally, conquer them. Remember you miss one hundred percent of the shots you never take. I have no fears about dating now. I've gone out enough to know how to make a date feel good and enjoy the date. Now, I'm ready to take on relationship fears I think…that's a whole different subset of concerns.

The Art of Kissing

I RECENTLY PICKED UP AN unread book I have on my bookshelf called **The Art of Kissing**. This small book by William Cane came from a neighbor's yard sale where I snagged it for only fifty cents. Probably the same yard sale where I bought the **Relationships for Dummies** book, too. Thank goodness, it wasn't a close neighbor.

The author starts out the book by reminding us of our first magical kiss. Think back; what was your first kiss like? Mine happened at church camp. Fourteen years old with braces, naturally I attracted another fourteen-year-old with braces. The other campers teased us that our braces would lock if we kissed. I guess we both gave a great deal of thought to that notion and decided to try it out. The result was my first kiss. While our braces didn't lock, there may have been some bruising from the braces. I can laugh at myself now because I know we were horrible kissers because we were clueless. Still, young people are supposed to start somewhere, but what if you're an adult and don't know how to kiss?

That's where **The Art of Kissing** comes in handy. Did you know smiling and laughing will garner you more kisses than looking sultry or sad? People are attracted to happy people...and they tend to kiss them, too. Don't know how to kiss? The author suggests placing your lips gently on your date's lips and waiting a few seconds, seeing if your sweetie will respond. Most will and then you follow their movements.

Different kisses mean different things. I went out on a second date with a guy where I was unsure if he liked me, but I liked him. At the end of the date, I received the sister kiss on the hair. What was that? What did it mean? I may have waved my hands in the air and yelled something about not being his sister. Still, it was sweet. It left me intrigued and willing to go out with him again. He later admitted that had been his intention to let me know he was fond of me, but not to press too hard too fast. It worked well since we still see each other.

William Cane reveals in his book that women love kissing. In fact, many women report they could do it for hours. The majority of women described kissing as being more intimate than sex. Most prostitutes refuse to kiss their clients because it is too personal. What makes kissing so special?

It brings a unique intimacy and warmness to a couple. You kiss people you both care about and love. It cements relationships. There is a hilarious scene in the movie **Leap Year** where all the older couples at the table are telling the "newlyweds" the secret of a good marriage. It is to kiss passionately every day, and then they demonstrate. They wait for the young couple to kiss. Their first kiss is an awkward peck because they don't really know each other. Then at the older couples' scoffing, they try again and really get into it. They discovered each other through kissing.

You can really tell a lot about a man from a simple kiss. To go from a kissing zero to hero he has to be creative. Men who kiss you in an unexpected location, such as on an escalator, are bound to get a reaction. Then, of course, there are men who kiss you on unexpected places. The number one place women like kisses beside the lips, according to Internet survey, is the neck.

What if a man is horrible at kissing? It could be he's a shy guy who hasn't had much experience, but might be willing to learn? Then, there are men who are rather rigid with their lips and just lean over and peck at you as if they were a chicken and you were a kernel of feed corn. That's not overly appealing. If a man has been married and is over thirty-five and he is still pecking at you...well, you may have to decide how much you like kissing compared to the guy's company. This is not someone who enjoys kissing. At best, he sees kissing as a way to warm up the woman for the main event. If he only knew, he wasn't warming her up.

In Cane's book, both men and women participated in a survey to see how Americans fared on the kissing scale. Okay ladies, I think you might know the answer. Europeans, especially Italians, French, and Spanish kissed more frequently and kissed well. They also kissed in public more and kissed for the sake of kissing. Sadly, even the Germans scored higher than Americans. We can take heart that our British cousins scored rather low, too. The complaints against American men included that they usually don't know how to kiss; they're too forceful, and they see it as only a prelude to sex. American women were not open to public kissing as much as their European cousins and didn't open their mouths as much. We can tell ourselves that was only the opinion of people answering the survey.

A man who loves to kiss and is willing to learn and experiment is priceless. He'll feather delicate kisses over his lover's closed eyes. Playful Eskimo nose rubs and puppy dog lick kisses are in his repertoire, along with lip sucking and French kissing. He's tried them all at some time and is willing to attempt more. Think back to all the romantic comedies you've watched. Do you remember a hero who was a terrible kisser? Probably not, I know I can't think of one.

The reason behind this is women want men who can kiss well. A kiss epitomizes romance. A man who kisses well and times his kisses appropriately can usually have his pick of women. A recent article on the **Life Gems for Marriage** website touts the ability of a single kiss to not only increase your bond but also relieve your stress level. After a hard day, a simple hug and kiss can make you feel SO much better. On the flip side, couples who divorce usually haven't kissed for a very long time. The lack of kissing helps break down their initial bond. They no long feel close because they're not. Never underestimate the power of a kiss.

What Scares Men The Most

A WOMAN WITH A CHILD scares off the average man. A woman with more than one child sends him running. Women tend to mumble about the man being a jerk when he avoids dating a mother with young children. Let's look at things from his side for a moment.

When I was expecting, I read several books about what to expect while pregnant. I knew all about water weight, midnight cravings, and false labor pain, but nothing about how the marital relationship would change.

The various books emphasized it would change, but not for the better for the man. Instead of being the lover and the hero, he's shoved to the side while the baby receives all the attention. Everyone fusses over the mother and the baby. Of course, most of you are saying the baby needs the attention. Newsflash: the man needs attention too. Suddenly, everything is about the child from sleeping patterns to social activities. The mother finds herself cuddling and kissing the baby so much she actually fulfills her need for physical touch. She has little need to caress her husband. When he wants affection, she's tired.

The man becomes the breadwinner and the shared caregiver to the child. He gets to escort the child around to various functions with little praise from the child or mother. The parents finally divorce because there is no connection and affection between the two of them. The mother is angry while often the father is relieved. Maybe this time he thinks, I'll find someone who has time for me; someone who will appreciate me for who I really am as opposed to some unpaid servant to the child or children. He also harbors tremendous guilt over leaving his children EVEN if the mother pushed him out.

What the divorced father sees when he meets a woman with children is the scenario he just left. He is well aware of what it's like to have three kids in three different activities, and only one car to get them there. As Americans, we seldom tell our children no and allow them to drive the marriage by default. Most people do not have marriages; they enter into a relationship, then have offspring and become slaves to those children, fulfilling their every want and even creating ones the children never ever had.

I witness this when I go to my spin class and watch parents mill around waiting for their pre-school karate students. Karate class meets three times a week and is quite pricey. The parents, instead of doing something useful like working out, wait two hours leaning against a wall. They probably don't have money left for a gym membership after paying for karate. They give up any leisure time waiting and almost all their discretionary funds to the child. This is what the man sees when a woman mentions she has a kid. The man probably has children he is already supporting and occasionally drives to activities.

If a man is honest, he'll also realize it will be a long time before they are a couple if ever. A mother's first responsibility is to her children, especially very young children. Teenagers can manage on their own enough to let mom date or enter into a relationship. A few will throw a nasty fit worthy of any Lifetime movie character that might make mom reconsider dating for a while. With mothers, everything is about the children. A romantic, weekend getaway suffers cancelation due to junior having the sniffles or his Little League team making it to regionals. If a woman doesn't cancel, then she criticized by other women for being a bad mother.

Men will enter into relationships with mothers because there are very few single women without kids. It may not be what he wants, but the woman seems eager at first, welcoming, even affectionate. Of course, while she may see an attractive, amusing man, she also sees help. What single mom doesn't need a hand? It would be great to have someone to lean on and pick up the kids from daycare. An extra income would help, too. These things tend to color how a woman reacts to the man, but it isn't love, and it definitely isn't a relationship. You can call it a relationship, even marriage, but it is only a name, not a fact.

What usually happens is the man enters the relationship with doubts, but figures it's the best he is going to do. He soon finds himself driving the mini-van and spending more time with the kids than the mother. Mom is so relieved to have help she's anxious to do all the things she couldn't do with kids and takes advantage of the newest member of the family. She'll even indulge in nights out with the girls because it has been so long, she explains to her bewildered man, who thought a relationship meant they spent time together.

The man falls into the child cycle where everything revolves around the child or children. His sporty car that doesn't allow two car seats into the back seat becomes unacceptable. His golf day or poker night interferes with the children's activities. The romantic getaways for two morph into theme parks visits with sunburned, whining children. Not the life he imagined; he could have stayed married to the mother of his children and had the same life. In fact, the staying married to his ex might start to look good; at least he would be raising his own children, not someone else's.

To pile even more abuse on the beleaguered man the children will tell him how great the absentee father is. If the woman has a cruel streak, which some often do, she might mention that her ex-husband or ex-boyfriends were good at everything from fixing cars and cooking to being amazing in the bedroom. She probably thinks throwing out these remarks will inspire the man to greater efforts. In the end, he realizes he doesn't matter in the relationship.

A man may find himself shelved after the kids grow up. He was good when the kids were small, but not the type of person the mother wanted with the kids grown. In other words, he was a satisfactory daddy, but not a lover. He may have felt the relationship go south soon after he said, "I do," but he stayed because he felt an obligation to her children. He served his purpose and now she's done with him. He feels just the same as before his initial divorce.

I can understand why a man would avoid the women with children. The woman's affection fades away under the challenges of childcare. Suddenly, he goes from a hero to a doofus who doesn't remember to buy milk and diapers on the way home. The number one cause of second marriages failing is children, according to marriage therapist Larry Bilotta. **Psychology Today** magazine states sixty percent of second marriages fail. This statistic is devastating for a man who already has one failed marriage behind him. Why would he want to take a chance on a relationship that only has a forty percent chance of success at best?

The obvious solution to all of this is to date an older woman whose children are grown. This woman is who she is going to be and will not change once the children leave since they already have left. Instead of a three-ring circus with half a T-ball team and a mini-van, romantic getaways are possibilities. Adult conversation is another benefit. It's all out there on the table. No secret desire to have more children is waiting in the wings.

Next time you bash a man for not wanting to date a woman with young children, think about his point of view for a change.

The Booty Call Date

THE RULE OF THUMB IS when you think it is a booty call date, then, it probably is. Some women second-guess themselves, wondering if they are maligning their date, thinking the worst of them. Here are a few hints:

1. No matter what you talk about, your date brings the conversation back to sex. If you ask if he has any pets, he tells you he likes it doggy-style. Of course, you change the subject, ignoring his innuendo.
2. He greets you with a kiss more appropriate if he had been at sea for the last six years.
3. He helps you with your coat or chair and manages to cop a feel in the process.
4. He tells you his ex-wife or previous girlfriend was cold in bed and he likes it hot. Do you remember ever asking about his ex in bed? I bet you didn't.
5. He compliments you on your toned body, suggesting you would be very limber in bed. Suddenly that compliment got completely yucky.
6. He stares at your cleavage even when you are not wearing a revealing top. He is just waiting for his X-ray vision to kick in which is a "side benefit" from the male enhancement drug he purchased.
7. He slips off his shoes and gets frisky under the table. This is a good time to jump up and scream "rat" or

"snake" either one should alert the manager and get you gone.

8. He hints that there is a handy motel close by or his apartment is near. Surprise! Could he have actually planned this?

9. He starts humming "Let's Get Drunk and Screw."

10. He encourages you to drink even after you told him you don't want anything else.

Ladies, don't take any of these signs as a compliment. Any willing female will do. If you are smart and walk out on him, he'll start on the waitress or the hostess. Beware of the follow-up phone call where he begs for forgiveness and another chance. Translation: I haven't gotten lucky with anyone else so I am willing to try some new techniques on you.

Newly divorced women and long-time single women should recognize a booty call for what it is. As much as you want it to be some sort of offering before your altar of feminine attractiveness or a prelude to a relationship, it isn't.

I asked a close, trusted male friend if a woman goes to bed with a man too soon, would he drop her because of no bedroom skills or would he keep her if she were good. His reply shocked me. He stated emphatically that the man would always stop seeing her. His only purpose was to get her into bed. Once that happens, the game is over. Really? I had to ask for confirmation. I always thought, as have many of you, if a woman were an amazing sexual dynamo the man would stay. While he stayed, a relationship would magically develop. I believe in wishing on falling stars, too.

He did qualify his statement, though, thank goodness! Otherwise, we'd have to give up on the male gender entirely. There are thoughtful, stable men who want a long-term relationship. They won't initiate sex on the first date, or for several weeks after that, and when they do, they are serious. No real problem with getting your booty call man confused with your thoughtful type.

Old boyfriends, even ex-husbands, can and do resort to a booty call. That call you get at the last minute or late at night when the guy just wants to come to your house to talk. Suggest IHOP or McDonalds for conversation, you'll be surprised how he doesn't want to talk anymore.

Don't get excited because your ex called. It is more likely he is between women, and you're a sure thing. Isn't there a reason he's an ex?

Then there's the sympathetic ploy where something awful has happened, and you're the only person who would understand. Translation: Sucker. Keep in mind; he has called everyone else he knows first before approaching you. He might even tell you that you're his last hope. Beware, this man knows you. He may have been scum when you were together, but he's also scum who remembers how kissing the back of your neck makes you hot. Don't let him come over.

A few of you will explain how you might get back together. You might, but you'll also break up again. Do you want that? You also might fall into a booty call relationship where he keeps showing up for sex and food. How do you know you're in a booty call relationship? If the man isn't wining and dining you or trying his best to woo you with extravagant gestures, then you are probably perilously close—if not already—in a booty relationship. It is especially telling if you never appear in public together, and I am talking about something more than Wal-Mart.

Now that it's been spelled out for you, you realized you

been the victim of a booty call or you're currently in a booty call relationship. If you want mindless sex with someone who doesn't care about you, feel free to continue. Keep in mind, all a man wants for a booty call is a willing female, preferably attractive, but definitely ready. If this sounds like you, drop him cold turkey. Don't be polite. Don't worry about him sticking around because he won't. Every now and then, he might text you between females, especially when he's drinking. Ignore it. It means nothing.

Now, you're ready to consider what you really want. Don't sigh over old hookups or booty calls. They never turn into worthwhile relationships. What would you have really? A man who was always trying to score with every female he encountered. Please, every woman deserves better than that.

Update: *Women can work this angle, too. Ask yourself if she wants to be seen in public with you? If not, you've become a friend with benefits. All the advantages are hers because she is looking for a man for a regular relationship, but using you to take the edge off.*

Clueless

ARE MEN CLUELESS OR IS it the women when it is come to the delicate science of romance and attraction? I guess that would depend on whom you talk to as a reference. My sweetie and I just finished watching **500 DAYS OF SUMMER**, a romantic comedy told from a male perspective. Tom, the main character, recalls his growing affection and eventual love for Summer, a new girl at work.

Tom does odd things, such as making cryptic comments to ordinary questions she asks to playing her favorite band on his laptop computer. As you can guess, Summer bops through her days unaware that Tom is crushing on her. My sweetie saw this and wondered why Summer didn't have a clue. Where was the clue I wondered aloud? We only notice what we are looking for.

If we're looking for something, then we rewrite the whole script to suit our theory. John Gottman, a renowned relationship expert, can gauge a marriage by the first met story. A happy couple tells a charming story filled with tenderness. The unhappy couple will tell a tale of bitterness with the wife practically snarling how she should have killed him when she met him. Both stories probably didn't happen exactly as portrayed, but were edited due to how the teller feels about their partner.

Tom, in the story, wants to fall helplessly in love while Summer is in the big city to have fun. Ladies, I think you know what is going to happen here. Reminds me of a Black Friday story where two people standing in line at Target for a couple of hours fell in love. Really? The woman or man who falls in love that fast falls in love with an idealized version of love, not the person. That's what Tom did.

I pointed out to my sweetie that Summer could be mean, moody, and selfish. He definitely agreed on the moody part because he believes women indulge in moodiness to justify bad behavior. We, the viewers, see these moments, but Tom, the desperate to be in love man, only sees loving glances and smiles. Any of you see yourself here?

Think of relationships you translated into something more. You couldn't understand why the man left you or maybe never asked you out to begin with because the two of you had something. That something may have been only in your mind. Tom asks his younger sister for advice. She advises him to ask Summer where he stands. The only problem with that, he explains, is what if she doesn't see me as her boyfriend? What do we do if what we believe does not measure up to reality? Then we have to give up the relationship, even if it only existed in our mind.

Too often, people want different types of relationships. Tom wanted to be wildly in love while Summer was content to have someone to hang out. You can't have a successful pairing when two people involved want two different relationships. This is probably more widespread than most people realize. Tom's date who listened to Tom gush about Summer, explained that the terms of his relationship with Summer were out front along. She didn't lie to him. He was the one who wanted more. Too often, we don't understand the terms of the relationship, and when we finally do, we realize we were the partner who wanted more or an entirely different relationship. We become angry for wasting so much time.

Our alternative is we can accept the first person who pays some attention to us, who could also turn out to be mentally unbalanced. As my sister likes to remind me, the crazy ones have no fear of rejection. That's why they approach you immediately. Even when rejected, they refuse to accept it and become stalkers. With this in mind, we have to try to meet people. We have to be out there with our clueless counterparts instead of accepting whoever shows up at our door.

It's hard to do the right thing. Our own insecurities hamper relationships. Tom asked Summer about her previous boyfriends, and she tries to not tell him, but he insists. He imagines each boyfriend, as more attractive, sexy, and talented than he is. How often have you've been guilty of this? It is a don't-go-there zone.

On the other hand, Tom engages in the same behavior once Summer dumps him. I laughed when Tom begins to explain to a date the great love he had for Summer. Tom was clueless why this might be inappropriate. Guys can't ever win if they talk about an old girl when out with a new one. If they trash the ex, then they sound bitter and challenging, not the type of person a woman would want to see again. If the man talks politely about his ex, emphasizing how she's a great person, then he comes across as being flighty because he didn't hold onto such an incredible female. You never win when you talk about your ex. All the time spent talking about an old love is time taken away from a potential love.

Summer and Tom meet again at a mutual friend's wedding. They sit together, dance together, and she invites him to her engagement party. She forgets to mention it is her engagement party. At the party, he questioned why she asked him to dance. Her response was she wanted to dance. He saw the dance as an opportunity to get back together. Once engaged, she harbored no romantic feelings for Tom, so a dance really was just a dance. Besides, she knew Tom would dance with her.

Our inability to read minds causes us to be clueless around the opposite sex. Sometimes we bring in friends, co-workers, even little sisters to give us their opinion of the situation. This only works if we can give a factual recounting as opposed to what we want to happen. Those men, who zero in on a girl at a party only to be blown off, then move on to another, maybe they're smarter than I initially thought. My first impression is they didn't really care about the women. They were just looking for someone who wasn't into anyone else.

It probably works better than longing for someone for months, building up fantasies about him, making walk-bys, giving longing looks he misses; only to find out he has a girlfriend in another state. Makes you wonder who is the more clueless—the ones who hit on anything that moves or the ones who build entire fantasy lives around people they are too shy to approach.

Update: *How much time do you really want to spend on someone? Instead of leaving cryptic clues, you could be dating someone who actually wants to go out with you.*

Attitude: What's Yours?

IN THE BOOK, **The Hidden World of Dogs** by Elizabeth Marshall Thomas, the author explains how a tiny poodle can chase a Great Dane from her yard. The little dog barks so hard her front feet come off the ground. She is serious, and the big dog knows it, which causes a retreat. I've seen it happen with my own opinionated, small dog. He tells my much larger dog what he can and cannot do. Dogs respect attitude, and the one with the most gets to be the alpha dog. What does this have to do with dating? Should we be barking in our front yards to get the attention we need?

Not hardly, but we do need to check our attitudes, literally. What is your attitude? How do you regard yourself? Your dating prospects? Are you aware you get what you believe you deserve to get? It is a form of self-fulfilling prophecy. How often have you gone out on a first date with the impression it will be a horrible date, and it was. If you started out with a negative attitude, you found every tiny thing you could criticize about your date if only in your mind. Trust me, he felt your negative energy and gave it back to you. You didn't put yourself out to be friendly because you'd already written your date off. On the other hand, he was probably busy trying to figure out how he could be shed of you. Do you need an attitude adjustment?

Yes, if you're feeling low about yourself and everything else. You attract people who reflect back the same attitude you hold about yourself. Think of Gilligan's Island for a moment, then think of cheerful, cute Mary Ann. I am Mary Ann...have been my entire life and hated the fact I wasn't, Ginger. I was so displeased over not being tall, slinky, and sultry that I didn't feel good about myself or even consider myself attractive. Guess what? I found plenty of people who would beat up on me too, telling me how unattractive or worthless I was.

My ex-husband was very fond of commenting on other women's attributes in front of me. Now, while I didn't have a high self-esteem, I am logical. I would be mystified that he thought someone was beautiful who didn't even have the basic features I possessed. Looking back, I remembered they did have attitude. They knew men were checking them out, and they viewed it as their tribute.

When I decided to change my attitude about myself, it was hard. I had to re-accept myself every day as I looked into the mirror. I verbalized what was good about me each day. I felt ridiculous when I first started, but after a while, I was willing to believe. Once I believed, I was attracting men who thought I was wonderful and beautiful, too. It's all in the attitude.

Some people just don't believe they are worthy of respect despite being incredible folks. A good example of this is a male friend who is allergic to cats, but his ex-wife and daughter insisted on keeping multiple cats. He even had the thankless job of cleaning out the cat box. How horrible. What the ex-wife was affirming with her behavior was she didn't value or respect him. Part of the reason was he didn't value himself or he would have pulled the plug on the whole cat scheme. It hurts me to think people are so thoughtless. As for the man, he turned in his cat box scoop along with his ex-wife. He also learned how to regard himself as being special and, in turn, attracted a very special lady.

I have heard so many women say there are no good men left in the world. With that attitude, do you think they will find any? Nope and they don't want to either. It would ruin their sour on men position. Same with the guys, you know the ones, convinced every woman is out to use them. They attract conniving women who use them. A better attitude would attract a higher caliber of female.

Your attitude affects so much about your life. A good mood actually keeps illnesses at bay. A smile on your face attracts people to you. Being positive also helps you be lucky at anything. Who do you prefer? The cheerful person or the emotional vampire who spends twenty minutes describing her various woes.

Positive emotion is a powerful force. It can definitely change minds, and other times it can even turn equipment on and off in scientific studies on paranormal abilities. Negative energy has no power except to bring you down. Get several upbeat people together and be ready to be amazed at their combined power. They really can do anything.

When I changed my attitude to men are lucky to go out with me, they felt and acted fortunate to be with me. I was still cute Mary Ann, but surprisingly, being Mary Ann was okay. I found plenty of men who were Mary Ann fans. It really is all about attitude.

Confessions: Teddybear36 Tells All

OKAY, LADIES, I KNOW WAY MORE than I should about online dating from a guy's point of view. Maybe I should say from what guys see. I didn't just get it from asking men because they will only tell me so much. You know, only the stuff that won't completely honk me off, especially if I were on a date with the guy when I asked. Here's the deal: I was *Teddybear36*.

A couple of years ago, I got mad at an ex-boyfriend. In my opinion, he was the template for everything wrong in a man. I didn't understand how such a fraud could meet women online. To test a hypothesis, I made up a profile for him as if I were him. Ladies, it was classic male, chauvinist pig all the way. *Teddybear36* liked to watch television, eat, smoke, and drink. He was looking for a young, leggy blonde to cater to him. If that wasn't bad enough, I made him retired, no hobbies, and no desire to go anywhere. Twisting the knife a little more, I mentioned that women were on this earth to look after men. The last sentence in the profile contained the fact that he owned a high-end car and was well off financially.

I even used a photo from the Internet, and it was not flattering at all. It was a picture of an overweight, unkempt man with his hair going gray and his jowls hanging down. Some of you may be wondering if I got any hits. Were there any women out there looking for a man who hates women, but would like to be serviced by one? Actually, I got about forty-two replies.

First, I weeded out the fake profiles, which included the beautiful, sweet things that lived far away. Eventually, they will ask for money so they can visit. When I worked in a locked down facility for young offenders, they used to make up these types of profiles all the time. They made sure the girls were always from a foreign country since their own English was questionable. Then it was on to the real profiles or what I thought was real.

Some women sent pictures of themselves in cleavage baring tops or swimsuits. Many were leaning forward or the photo was shot at a downward angle to make the girls appear larger. As a woman, I knew that trick. Women who send pictures of the girls or their booty tragically think that is all they have to offer.

Women also post old photos. As a woman, I could recognize hairstyles that have been out of style for at least twenty years. Maybe a man might think something was wrong but couldn't put his finger on it.

Not all my hopeful dates were young. Some were way out of the ballpark as far as what I considered an appropriate age. They wrote to me about the disgustingly graphic things they would do to please me. Why the porn filter did not block that I don't know. How it passed over the woman who painted herself as opposed to wearing a swimsuit—I am unsure about that, too. Some of the replies I got were very skanky. I felt the need to disinfect my laptop. I had no doubt that these sexual offers were directly connected to *Teddybear36* being financially well off. Others may have thought they could get a ring on his finger before feeding *Teddybear36* some anti-freeze laced lime Jell-O.

The reply from a widow who said I reminded her of her husband broke my heart. He wasn't the best man in the world, she wrote, but she loved him. All she wanted was to find someone else to look after since he was gone. My *Teddybear36* guy would never contact her because she was too old, not leggy blonde material at all.

Then there was one average person. She admitted she was new in town and didn't think they would suit romantically, but could still hang out. Her profile listed a range of degrees and hobbies. Her photo was cute too, but still too old for finicky *Teddybear36's* taste. I thought she sounded like a wonderful person. I was tempted to write her as myself, but how would I explain that I was a woman pretending to be a man out of spite? I did learn what the other women were putting out there. I am also happy to report most women were smart enough not to respond to *Teddybear36*.

One of the most glaring points of my whole experience was that my profile wasn't checked by the agency. No one checked to see if I was married, a felon, retired, or even a guy. I learned some women would throw themselves at you if you have money. Online hopefuls should try to meet as soon as possible because men can become creative on their profile, too. Usually, they add two to three inches to their height and subtract five years from their age. They also manage to find photos where their hair is still luxuriously thick. It is better to meet the real man as opposed to the fantasy one you'll create in your head the longer you put off the actual meeting.

Strangely, after seeing what other women did on their profiles, it didn't cause me to change my profile. I figured half those women would not deliver on what they were promising, but hoped to get their foot in the door.

A word of caution to online daters: be suspicious of a man who writes like a woman. All sorts of people make profiles like felons, teenagers, even hurt women. eHarmony recently offered a verification service where they check the client out to see if he is using his real name, age, occupation, and marital status. This actually allows men to date up the dating ladder because more quality women will pick the site over others because they trust it. The man must opt for the verification process, though. Makes you wonder when they don't.

Malcolm, my trusted male friend, informed me that men don't bother with the verification process since it is another expense on top of an already high monthly fee.

The Pickup Artist

MOVIES HAVE EXEMPLIFIED THE pick-up artist as being the ultimate smooth guy who manages to draw women in with left-handed compliments. What man doesn't envy Mr. Suave and Debonair? Apparently, many do, so much so, they are watching shows and taking classes on how to be a hunter in the dating game.

VH1 had its own show called **The Pick Up Artist**. On the show, a sexually ambiguous man prances around in high heel boots and eyeliner and gives advice to other men. This show amused me because I was not sure if the star even liked women, let alone would be capable of picking one up. VH1 knew a moneymaking topic even if their star was different from your traditional alpha male. The fact that the show only lasted two seasons to disappointing reviews suggested that I wasn't the only one having a hard time believing women would actually be attracted to Mystery, the high heel-wearing instructor.

Many men have written books and developed websites about picking up women. Web sites featuring photos of scantily clad, busty women with various come on lines lure the hopeful male into learning how to seduce women. These sites remind me of all the different online dating website teasers that show half a dozen model-like individuals waiting to meet you. Most people are well aware that no one like that lives in their city...and yet they want to believe.

They wish those models wanted to date them just as if they want to think they can pick them up, too. All it really takes is money to buy the needed information.

On a **Criminal Minds** episode, they profiled a killer who used a pickup artist class to meet his victims. The instructor informed his students to be different from other men. It included wearing hats, glasses, colored contacts, even eye patches to stand out from the other men. The would be pick up artist/serial killer resorts to pitting two women against each other by paying attention to one, then ignoring her for her friend. This wins women over. How drunk do they really have to be?

My own sweetheart paid good money for a pickup artist course. He joined the thousands of other men who believed there was a secret formula for meeting and winning women. Not every bit of advice he read worked with me. He held back and acted as if he wasn't interested in me when we first met because the great online guru advised him that showing too much interest would drive me away. What happened is I felt he wasn't interested in me. By playing it cool, he chased me away. Luckily, since I was dating other guys, I just let it ride and went out with the other men.

He was following the advice he read online. It was supposed to drive me wild with desire. Instead, I felt he didn't like me—which pushed me into dating additional men. Ironically, much later, he told me when he met me; he knew I was the one. He even gave himself the mental speech not to screw up. His efforts included waiting to call me after our first date. It would look uncool according to his online coach if he called too soon. I thought it made him look like he didn't care. I was miffed and hurt a little. Usually, I heard from a guy immediately after the first date. One dating site even told me it was protocol to follow up the first date with a phone call within 24 hours. The length of time a guy lingered signaled his disinterest. By this time, I was sure I was old news. When he did call days later, I was puzzled.

By following the pickup artist's advice, he pushed me away with both hands. What he didn't realize was there were men who were willing to confess to liking me a lot on a first date. They'd press for a second date immediately or call me after I got home from the first date to make sure I was okay and to re-establish contact. They were doing all the things the pick-up artist had warned would look needy and desperate. Personally, I found them sweet gestures.

Most of you are wondering why I ever continued to see a guy who awkwardly followed some online advice king. I saw flashes of who he was when he wasn't trying to follow some script. I also sensed he was putting up a façade that wasn't really him. The tiny flashes I saw intrigued me, and I wanted to know more.

We laugh now about the mixed messages and awkward courtship. He was uncertain if I liked him even on our fifth date. Women seldom make it to a fifth date with men they do not like. Luckily, my sweetie gave up on the pickup artist's advice by date three. I am so glad he did. I'm unsure how much more I would have willingly tolerated. After all, how much does a pickup specialist, who has never met me, know about me? Nothing. I do not fit into one of online pickup guru's tidy categories.

I pointed out to my sweetie that the pickup artists work in bars where women drink heavily and are willing to fall for any man. They've strapped their beer goggles on and view most men favorably, especially as the hour grows later. The pickup artists never give superb advice for meeting women at observatories, libraries, or even Renaissance fairs. The pickup artist is not out for a relationship, but a one-night stand. Maybe these odd behaviors will get him what he wants with someone drunk or stupid enough, or both.

As for me, I am just glad my sweetie smartened up and decided to be himself.

Dating Momma's Boy

AVOID ANY MOMMA'S BOY if you want any type of a prolonged, romantic relationship. Men who jump to do their mother's bidding earn the moniker Momma's Boy. Just a phone call from dear old mom has them switching their date night or dropping the girl altogether to rush to transplant mommy's geraniums which have become a bit root-bound. Mother has first claim no matter what, and marriage doesn't diminish her rights. Any woman who hooks up with this devoted son will have to settle for being second best.

Women do stumble into relationships with momma's boys because they are such thoughtful men. Who doesn't respect a son who treats his mother well? It is certainly better than a man who treats his mother with contempt. The alarm bells may start to go off when Mom stands as an authority on everything from cooking to dating etiquette. You should run very fast if he wants Mom to take you shopping so she can give you some fashion tips. You may have just landed a starring role in a reality horror show.

There are endless television shows that employ at least one character with an overbearing mother. **The Big Bang Theory** is a good example. One of its super smart characters lives with dear old mom who only wants the best for her son. One episode featured Mom yelling helpful advice from the other side of the bedroom door when her son snuck a girlfriend home. She even apologizes for her son's lack of sexual stamina and asks the girl to give him another chance. We laugh because no one is like that—or are they? I dropped a man who adored me. He was good looking, polite, and charming. People liked him, but I decided he and his mother were much too close when he told me his mom discussed her sex life with him on a regular basis.

Most women do not enjoy dating men who keep in regular contact with their exes. It is especially distasteful when he compares you to the ex. This gets old fast. It is nothing beside the mother test. Be prepared for the momma's boy because his mother is the best. She is the gold standard for everything from cooking to spoiling her boy rotten. Why shouldn't he favor his mother? She bought his adoration by exceptional indulgence, sometimes to the point of neglecting other siblings or her spouse.

Can you think of an ex who seemed especially spoiled? He not only expected you to wait on him but his mother, too. If so, you may have encountered the classic edition of the momma's boy. This version believes that being male is the pinnacle of social evolution. Women are supposed to wait on this man because that is their purpose in life. A colleague explained to me that she had to clean her brother's room every day because she was a female. Her brother did nothing because it was woman's work. Her mother enforced this edict, making her into an epitome of the perfect woman in the son's eyes. This type of man will not view women as being equal to men. Ironically, a woman shaped this belief.

Momma's boys evolve in a variety of ways, rather like a science experiment gone wrong. Everyone is aware that it is wrong to favor one offspring over another. What happens when you do? You can end up with a momma's boy or a daddy's girl depending on the sex of the child and parent.

One mother who had several daughters, one son, and a husband she had long given up on loving, decided to use the son as her tool. The husband had insisted on more babies until the long awaited son was finally born. The mother, who was vengeful used the son to exact her revenge. She preferred the son to her daughters. He was perfect in her eyes and did little to help around the household. In small family disputes, he always got his way. The mother bought him special treats the other children didn't receive to bind him to her as opposed to the father. The result was he had little to do with his father, whom his mother despised. His sisters hated him, and he expected everything his way.

In today's world, we are creating more financial momma's boys. I can remember being a teen and planning to move out. I had my first apartment at eighteen, and no one I knew stayed at home past twenty-one. The average age of the unmarried, American male leaving home currently is twenty-nine, and many stay longer. Why not? Mother makes it easy with regular meals, laundry service, and few financial demands. This type of dependence stymies emotional growth. Even after the man physically leaves, his mother still holds the financial purse strings often paying rent or buying groceries for her son who can't quite get it together. He has no reason to get it together as long as mother pays. What she is really paying for is a continued relationship based on obligation.

The momma's boy syndrome is problematic. A woman who has carefully crafted her son into a drone to continually serve her is a very needy and controlling woman. She will expect to control you, too. At first, she may seem very nice, but you haven't crossed her yet. You haven't challenged her authority or made her son choose between the two of you.

Newsflash: he will always choose her because she will always be there for him. Those other women merely pass through his life, never staying. Do you even have to wonder why?

Going Ugly

WHEN I FIRST READ THE headline that another journalist accused Author Vicki Larson of urging women to go ugly, I figured she told women not to wear makeup to the grocery store. Nope, her crusade emphasized the importance of passing over your male model types in her recent article, "Hot or Not? Why Women Shouldn't Pick Attractive Husbands." The article was a response to famous men, known more for their bodies and sexuality than common sense and decency, who were in recent headlines.

In her article, she readily admits that most women go for the over-confident male, sure of himself and his charm. Larson also adds that money and power inserted into the mix makes a physically average or below average man extraordinarily attractive to women. The men, often because of their prominence, can have any woman they want, and they do. Women vie for their attention because they believe to get it is a real mark of recognition.

This same man will eventually get to all the women in the room. That is his way because he must have continual feminine adoration. A good example of this is a high profile senator. While separated from his wife and obviously had a girlfriend on the side—he was still hitting on girls at a college bar near his apartment at the same time. This is what your average pretty boy does. Since he was a youngster, females have fawned all over his beauty, commenting on it, giving him extra chances because he was so cute when the average male would be history.

Larson warns women who pursue high-profile men that they may be hurt in the end. Look at Joe Ordinary. He isn't ugly either as the original title might imply. Your average guy never grew up gorgeous. Instead, he had bad haircuts, braces, and glasses. He may have even struggled with his weight and his self-esteem, but that allowed him to develop a personality and empathy. My sister theorizes that beautiful people never have to learn to play well with others because being beautiful was enough. While the rest of us are trying to be funny, original, or smart to attract the opposite sex, they just exist as a force of nature.

It is odd how we criticize men for pursuing beautiful, but often mercenary, women while women turn around and do the same thing with men. What do you get when you attempt to trap the male equivalent of the supermodel? Out of the two thousand plus comments on Larson's article, the general theme was the same. Over the top men do not really care about women they date. All their relationships occur at a superficial level where they live their life. While most of the women who commented swore off pretty boys, the men's comments were more telling.

Men who tried to be decent, caring individuals were regularly steamrolled by the handsome set who took their girlfriends, and often their wives, as they rolled by. Their cries of anguish were as loud as the women's voices, but even more embittered, as they should be. Your average guy provided a stable, loving relationship with his sweetheart. He endured chick flicks with her, took out the garbage, mowed the grass, and pretended to act pleased about her new haircut even when he wasn't. All of this adds up to nothing when Mr. Hot Bod wanders onto the scene with an abundance of charisma and well-defined biceps. The men felt like they gave all they had and yet were dismissed for a guy who gave nothing.

Larson advises the women to smarten up, learn from other women's experience. There are plenty of public examples out there. It really gets down to supply and demand. An abundance of dates tends to make any date not that special. Imagine trying to outdo the last four hundred dates. It can't be done. The beautiful people tend to discard people similar to used tissues.

The flipside to chasing a gorgeous guy, which you know is a bad deal, is having a man chase you, thinking you're fabulous. Men often base part of their personal value on how attractive their mate is. A prettier girlfriend makes a man feel good, which makes him treat her better.

According to Journal of Family Psychology, dating a less attractive man, may lead to a happier relationship.

"It's possible that a man who is less attractive than his partner feels so grateful to be with her that he works harder to maintain the relationship, amping up the amount of emotional support and kindness he provides," says Benjamin R. Karney, Ph.D., a professor of social psychology at UCLA. "Yet a man who is better looking than his partner knows he has lots of other options besides his mate, so he's less committed to providing the emotional support long-term relationships need to thrive."

Personally, I think the behavior your extra handsome men engage in is ugly. There are even more compelling reasons to date average, according to the journal.

"…you may find that your not-so-pretty man brings his A-game in the bedroom. 'What I've seen from my clinical practice is that women who are married to men less attractive than them often

have happy sex lives most likely because their mate tries harder to please them sexually,' says Bethany Marshall, Ph.D."

Bruno Mars sings about his girlfriend not seeing how beautiful she is through his eyes. We all assume his girlfriend is drop dead gorgeous. Maybe, maybe not, but it is how he sees her. It's the same with your man. If you love him and he's good to you, then he's gorgeous. Other people may not see him the same way because they haven't had the same experience.

The Dirt on Men

REAL QUESTIONS WITH REAL MEN ANSWERS.

Okay ladies, I have some burning questions that some of you want to know the answers. I have bona fide male responses from intelligent men. Maybe your man won't always match up, but the answers shocked me.

1. Does a man know when a woman is interested in him?

Sometimes, but usually not. Men aren't great ones to notice nuances like a woman. If a man isn't the confident bad boy who thinks every woman is after him, he may mistake your eye contact and cheery hellos for just being friendly, nothing more. Sometimes you just have to be more upfront, ask him out for coffee. Even then, he still might not get it, especially if he's an engineer.

2. Do men go out with women for the sole purpose of having sex?

Some do, and you should recognize them immediately. Despite all the movies, most men will not jump in bed with a woman because the men have fears, too. Yes, men worry about their bodies and performance. Most men realize if they sleep with a woman, she thinks it automatically means a relationship. Remember, men can and do have sex with women they do not like and never want to see again. They do it for one simple reason; the woman is offering.

3. Do men only date women they can see themselves having sex with or a possible relationship?

Men are not your gay best friend. They do not want to hang with you. A man will date a woman a couple of times to get a feel for her. If there is a third date, it is a deciding moment when he decides to pursue a relationship with you. That's why men get mad if you stop seeing them after the third date. They feel like they picked you, but you didn't pick them back.

4. How important are looks to a guy?

This is a tricky question. Men don't want model-thin girls. In general, men want to feel like they're the guy, and he's out with a girl. Dress like a female, a classy one. Wear a dress, fix your hair, put on makeup. This attracts the male eye. Don't dress like a skank. If you dress like a 'ho, you will be treated like a 'ho. Men who are looking for relationship material want a woman who looks well-groomed, not like someone who has a turnstile on her bedroom door.

5. Does a man want someone at the same education level or job level as himself?

This doesn't matter as much to a man as it does to a woman. Part of the reason is that a man takes care of himself. He isn't expecting to find a woman with a good job to take care of him. Honestly, you can only endure a dim bulb for so long. Smart men should avoid women who barely managed to snag a GED.

6. How does a man feel about a woman who already has children?

This depends on the person. Some men who never had children prefer a woman with children to give them the fatherhood experience. It depends on how active your ex is in your life and what is the level of conflict. No man wants to deal with an ex where the kids are always throwing how great their father is in his face. Most men, especially older ones, would prefer no children. Their reasoning is that they raised their children, and they definitely do not want to raise another man's.

7. How do men feel about sex in the relationship? When do they expect it?

Men expect sex in a relationship. Do not push sex as a way to get a man to commit since it will backfire. Sex needs to wait until you know the other person well. How long this takes differs, but it isn't the third date. Yes, men will leave after having sex with you and not because you were bad at it. That is the way some men are—they're players. If you waited to get to know them, you'd know this. Men respect women they have to wait for because they are the prize. Think of it like food. You can go to McDonalds and get something quick anytime of the day or you can go to an elegant restaurant. With the restaurant you make reservations, you plan, you anticipate going, you dress up, you savor the food, you linger, and then you remember the experience later. Do you want it to be McDonalds or an elegant restaurant?

Men really don't care what you look like naked. I know women don't believe this. Women worry that a man might focus on her large rear. Bring enthusiasm with you into the bedroom, and that's all the man notices. A man wants a woman who is excited to be with him. Nothing kills a man's ardor like the martyr babe who is doing it just because he wants it.

8. What does a man want in a long time partner?

A person that will support him emotionally. A woman who thinks he really is the greatest guy in the world. A man can find people to tell him how he screwed up. He even tells himself that. What he needs in a relationship is that one person who has his back. Men want an equal partner. There is much to recommend with the two wage-earner family.

Men are usually looking for someone with similar values and outlooks. If you are bemoaning your brown hair, dying it or highlighting it to attract a man, then stop. More men marry brunettes than any other hair color.

First Date Behavior

FIRST DATE BEHAVIOR MIGHT BE keeping us all single or at least uncomfortable on our dates. Writer John D. Husband in his book, **Single over Thirty,** notes an alien might watch all the single men and women go to various places that cater to singles, even meet up for a drink or dinner, then all return to their individual homes. The aliens wouldn't understand why two people who so much want to be part of a couple fail repeatedly. Everyone has a story.

When asked, both men and women have experienced bad first dates, usually due to incredibly rude behavior from their companion. Painful first dates linger in people's minds, causing them to talk about them and often mentioning the date by name. If you are that bad first date, it could be the reason behind your solitary state.

Many women and a few men walk into a first date believing they'll make the love connection that night. Five minutes into the date one or the other of them makes the mental decision it isn't going to happen. Where you go from there is what really counts. You could have a good dinner and conversation or create an ordeal that equals a root canal without anesthesia.

Often, dates don't look like their profile pictures or even dress appropriately for the event. Give them some slack. You may not resemble your photo, either. How would you feel if someone spent the entire night talking about your photo and how you didn't look anywhere close to it? Some people choose to do that with behavior instead of words by acting bored, looking at the clock, reading texts, even yawning. This same person makes no effort to be an interesting companion because he or she wrote you off at hello. How incredibly rude and stupid and presumptuous, assuming we all live in a bubble. Don't make the mistake of thinking rumors of your bad behavior will not reach other people or potential dates. It does. A waiter warned me off about a date after seeing how he treated previous women at the same restaurant.

How should you act on a date? You act as if you want to be there. You should be courteous, on your company behavior. Think of it as a trial run if you must. Remember the other person deserves a decent shot, even if he or she does not end up being the love of your life. Do you think you'll know on the first date? Most of us believe that our lives will unfold similarly to a movie script. I've met the love of my life, and I didn't realize it on the first date.

We met at a favorite restaurant, taking care of the security issue. We both dressed appropriately for our date. We didn't engage in heavy drinking or rowdy behavior. We didn't take phone calls, and we made entertaining conversation, or at least I thought I did. The result was a second follow-up date with someone I regarded as a nice guy. This should really be our aim as opposed to finding the love of our life in one night.

First dates are not for personal grilling as if you're an FBI profiler. Personal topics such as ability to father future children, getting married, and threesomes are off-limits. Ladies, it is not okay to ask the guy how much he makes. Would you like it if he asked how much you weighed? Exes are never good conversational topics. Save politics and religion for another day, too. Keep your conversation light and low key. Do you want people you don't know prying into your personal life? You probably don't enjoy your relatives doing this, so why put your date through this?

First dates are for getting to know the person well enough to find out if you'd be interested in knowing more. This isn't possible when you make the decision not to play your part in the conversation. If you had plans for acting this way, if the person didn't prove to be your real love, then you probably should have never accepted the invitation. The sad truth is your true love will take a pass on you and your rude date behavior. Trust me; this type of info does get around.

If you think your date is horrible, don't take it on yourself to tell him or her everything that is wrong. You will not be helping. In fact, you'll be little more than a bully.

Your date went through some of the same fears as you getting ready for your date. He may have harbored the same hopes that you might be the one. He could have suffered a similar disappointment that you weren't as charming in person as in emails. For one moment in time, two single people agreed to go out on a date with the presumption of having a good time. You can have a good time, treat each other well, and agree to part amicably.

Everything does not have to be a big drama where you bemoan your fate at being matched up with a loser. You chose to go out on the date. Make the best of it because you never know if your date has a sibling, a cousin, or a co-worker who would be perfect for you.

A Man's View on
Long Term Relationships

SO FAR, I'VE MAINLY COVERED dating from a woman's point of view. Today, I've had a courageous and frank male volunteer I'll call Malcolm, who is going to give his take on dating. Let me preface this by observing that Malcolm is an attractive, professional man in his mid-forties.

Malcolm's Take...

Even though women may not believe it, there are plenty of men looking for a lifetime companion. I know I am not the only one. The trouble is meeting professional, mentally stable women with grown or almost grown children in roughly my age bracket. Random chance, where I bump into my future mate in line at the post office, hasn't happened yet. To facilitate my search for a lifetime companion, I went online. In fact, I visited multiple dating sites, which cost me plenty.

The very fact women would judge me on a photo and a profile was intimidating. Women would decide on a few words and a somewhat unflattering snapshot if they wanted to meet me. It would probably take the average woman five seconds to decide if I were possible dating material. It would take a woman longer to decide between a pair of shoes. I swallowed my pride and asked a long time, female co-worker for her advice in helping to draft my initial profile. Unfortunately, after my friend tweaked my profile, it sounded like a woman wrote it. I trimmed the verbose profile until it sounded like a man, taking out words like *wonderful* and *beautiful.*

As a result of being on multiple sites, I usually received two matches a day. Often the sites sent me women that were too far away or simply out of my age bracket. The sites often ignored age and distance parameters just to match me. This resulted in one possible match per week that I would consider pursuing. Even though I sent out reasonable inquiries, I usually heard from only one woman a month. Because I didn't hear from the women I messaged, I often felt rejected. Even a note from a possible prospect saying, "thanks, but no thanks," would have been better than silence. The best I ever did was to get one woman per month to respond to my initial dating questions.

Once I started a conversation with a woman, she often dropped all communication within a week without explanation. This up and down ride of hopefulness and rejection caused me to disable my profile several times. Since random chance wasn't working, I went back and re-established my profile in another flurry of hope of meeting "the one." In my next attempt, I managed to keep a prolonged email relationship with a woman. I usually gave the woman my number with an invitation to call by the third email. If I made it to the phone call, then I could usually make it to the first date.

To prepare for my first meeting, I read Internet advice, which suggested a coffee date to avoid wasting money. This didn't appeal to my romantic nature and seemed a bit cold, so I opted for a regular sit-down type dinner. I worked very hard to prepare myself for the date, including studying my date's profile and thinking of conversational topics. Most of my dates were interesting, a few bizarre, and I enjoyed them for the most part. Unfortunately, there was no chemistry on the majority of my dates. A few let me know on the first date that there was no chemistry for them, either. While another few let me know they wanted to continue to see me, I didn't feel the same way about them. Then there were the others who made it to the second date by mutual agreement.

The second date involved more profile research and more conversation. I tried to find out more about family and personal likes and dislikes. By this time, I had been conversing back and forth by email, text, and phone. Sometimes the weirdness shows itself by this time. A good example of this was one woman stated she had one high school aged child on her profile. By the second meeting, she confessed to having four additional children that she failed to put on her profile. Her lack of honesty made me question everything else she had told me.

If I successfully made it past the second date, I had to think very carefully how I wanted to proceed. The third date from a man's point of view means he's interested in pursuing a relationship. Sometimes I didn't make it to the third date because it didn't feel right. I followed it up with a polite letter explaining that I had a good time but didn't feel like we would be a good match. Once the response to my letter was a hate-filled, email rant. This hurt because I worked hard to be a good date and a gentleman. Two dates does not a relationship make.

The main reason a guy doesn't show extreme interest on the first or second date is because it makes him appear needy and desperate. This type of behavior frequently turns off the confident woman I was hoping to attract. By the third date, the man realizes he can be considered possible boyfriend material if his date is interested in dating exclusively.

Most of the advice I'd read advised dating for three months before dating one person only.

While I did start several relationships, they fell apart for various reasons, someone in the past, some addictions, and some very lame excuses such as going to find herself. (Are you kidding me? You're in your late forties, where have you been?) I would have respected them more if they told me the truth.

Women often think men have it easy when it comes to dating. Most men have good intentions and do want to find that special someone and make her happy. Men have the same fears as women including their appearance, rejection, and being alone. Men do want a happily ever after ending.

I have to admit, however, that my system did finally work. Though I had many disappointments along the way, I finally found a woman online who does measure up to my high standards. A woman I treasure and can't wait to be with at the end of the day. We had some bumps at the beginning I will admit, but what good relationship doesn't start out rocky and unsure? I'm glad I hung in there, or I would have missed the most incredible connection a man could ever have with a woman.

It makes getting up in the morning a little easier to handle when you have a future to look forward to with a special someone. Is there still work to do? Of course! Any good relationship involves constant care and maintenance. In case you were wondering, my significant Sweetie is the author of this blog you've been perusing.

Oversharing

HAVE YOU EVER BEEN PART of a conversation when a person over shared? It makes you think of the person in an entirely different way, usually not favorable. Often we would rather not know certain things. Once we establish a connection, we'll do an immediate about-face, insisting on knowing all. Even concluding that the other person should confess their past loves to demonstrate their love. Such behavior is really a form of harassment. If a co-worker, as opposed to a romantic partner, insisted on such behavior, you'd refer to it as coercion or bullying. It sets a dangerous precedent of having to prove your love.

If you're the one begging to know all the details, be aware you'll not like what you hear. Of course, your man fell in love with other women before you. Some of them he may have fallen hard for and chased after them. Not all his relationships were horrible. There were women that treated him well. Do you really want to know this? Do you want to know that he spent an incredible weekend in Panama City with a former girlfriend as you head out for Florida?

Men and women believe they can judge a person's future potential by looking at their past relationships. I had a man query me about my divorce and decided I didn't present a strong enough case for the divorce and opted out of a date. Trust me, after that grueling interrogation worthy of the FBI, I didn't want to date him, either. Often, we as women try to decide if a man is worth our time by deciding who he dated in the past. There are major flaws with this type of rationale.

Whenever we tell our account of anything, it usually favors us in one way or another. We see it from our viewpoint, and we also see it in hindsight. It makes for a biased tale that is for the most part isn't correct or even flattering. You may tell your current squeeze the man before him was worthless with no redeeming features whatsoever. This might make him think you have a low opinion of all men. You aren't much of a prize or you would pick better men. It might make him feel not so great either.

Too much information taints everything. Recently while watching **The Big Bang Theory**, a drunken Raj decides to relate all the sexual misadventures of the bridegroom, Howard, unaware he's being taped. The bride viewed the YouTube gem and refused to have anything to do with her future husband. Because it was a television show, they managed to patch it up by Howard confessing he was no longer that despicable man. When you get right down to it, none of us are the people we were in the past. We've changed because of our experiences and choices, usually for the better. Do you want to be judged by your worst dating experience?

Then, on the other hand, you do need to know some things. Some vital information you should share.

1. Communicable diseases-men lie about this, especially STDs.
2. A number of times married, current marital status, and children.
3. Pending legal cases because this might end up costing you financially and emotionally if it goes on forever.

4. Food Allergies-Not too big of a deal, you just don't want to whip up something that might put him in the hospital.

5. Criminal record. Trust me; this can have an enormous impact on you. You might end up supporting him or being an accessory to a crime.

6. Religious/political outlook. Opposites might attract at first, but in the end you'll just consider one another deluded or brainwashed, which doesn't bode well for the length or happiness of the union.

7. Desire to have/or not have children. People assume too much when it comes to this.

8. Finances, including a credit score. I am amazed at how many people do not have a clue about what their spouse makes. They also are unaware how the money is spent. If you are dating a big spender, and you're a penny pincher don't expect things to work out well since you'll always argue about money. A low credit score can keep you from acquiring your own home or a new car at the optimum finance rate.

Watch what you share because it might cause problems down the road. Forget Joe Friday, who asked just for the facts. There are events you share with your girlfriends, then there are facts you share with your guy. Your girlfriends might like to talk about old beaus; your man doesn't. He also doesn't want to hear about previous weddings, proms, or the great shoes you just bought. The information that concerns him is about the two of you. It makes sense. Do you want to hear about all the great things he and a previous girlfriend did, even if he promised to do the same things with you? Yeah, that's what I thought.

If Opposites Attract, What do Likes Do?

EVERYONE KNOWS AT LEAST ONE person who is married to their polar opposite, a living example of opposites attracting. Why do opposites attract? When someone is so far out of your norm, you become curious. They are exotic, more like a movie star or an exchange student than a regular Joe. Their unusual habits, accent, or appearance initially brings out the novelty seekers, but different isn't always a good thing.

We love to hear stories about playboys who settle down with the girl next door. We usually only hear the first part of the story. We don't stay for the rest of the story where we'd have found out he settles down with about a dozen girls next door because they were so easy to fool. Many times when the hormones start calling, we are not comparing shared backgrounds.

You have sports fiends dating academic types who have never watched a playoff game in their lives. When the first rush of lust wears off and Angela Readsalot looks at the ridiculous lump on her couch, complete with foam cheese-head, screaming at the television, and swears off alcohol since they met in a bar. You probably know more couples that are ill-suited than couples who are well suited. Think about it for a minute. How did they get together? Most of you would think they fell in love, and I would agree with you. Did it ever occur to you that it takes more than love to make a relationship work out? (I know I am committing romantic heresy by suggesting this.) We expect one word that stands for ephemeral feeling that can't be touched to do all the work of a relationship. As my grandfather would say, that dog won't hunt.

So what do you do? In several countries, your parents engage in securing you an arranged marriage. This isn't a little project either. A marriage broker or matchmaker is consulted. The first thing she does is take a personal history of the client finding out all her likes and dislikes. Not too unlike dating websites with a big exception—matchmakers are not only matching you on twenty-seven connection points but on almost every one you can conceivably have. It doesn't mean the arranged match will have all of them. I never had a date that met all my twenty-seven connection points, either.

On a **20/20** special I watched, one Indian woman advertise for a man. Her ad was in about 10 pt. font and covered an entire newspaper page. It told her basic life story, the condensed version. It also stated what she was looking for in a man, including his financial prospects and willingness to relocate to the United States. Just imagine how much online dating services would charge for that type of an ad.

In arranging the match, the brokers try to connect the people on similarities, not differences. If she is from a middle-class family, then they look for a guy who is from a middle-class family. If she is college educated, then they look for someone who is college educated. The similarities automatically bind them together, when they don't really know each other well in the beginning. I like dating someone with similarities because they can get me. They understand many things about my life without me explaining because they had such a similar life.

The problem with dating opposites is you don't always agree with their lifestyles choices. Often what is normal to them just seems weird or wrong to you. You also spend a great deal of time explaining your life choices, because they are so different from your date's. Sometimes you feel forced to validate your own likes as if they needed validation. Worse is when you hide your own preferences and just go along with whatever your date wants, an appalling precedent. You can see why people with similarities offer a degree of comfort.

Going back to the Indian woman, her parents interviewed the parents of hopeful prospects. The couple wasn't even involved yet. Her parents picked out three men whom she met briefly on individual chaperoned dates to see if she liked any of them. She decided on one. The story picks up a year after their wedding with the bride confessing how much she loves her husband. Could this love have been obtainable by picking up a likely looking man at the country-western bar? It could happen if we're talking movie plot lines.

Men, at least the honest ones, will tell you they select dates initially on appearance. A man will keep dating the same person because of how she makes him feel as opposed to her appearance. A beautiful, but whiny, girl will eventually find herself shelved by a confident man. One of the things a man might find attractive about a date is their shared background, although he doesn't realize it at first. The sense of normalcy and calmness is because of how much they are alike.

So how do similar people match up, considering most believe opposites attract? I think like-minded individuals for a stable relationship. You're not busy re-inventing the wheel all the time because you're both familiar with it.

I dated a man once who loved his family. I love mine, but he LOVED his. They always ate Sunday dinner together. He would look for opportunities every day to run over and see his brother and sister. He really enjoyed this. From my point of view, it was a form of torture listening to them talk about people I didn't know and drink themselves into a maudlin stupor.

My preferred date would see his family only on the main holidays. Before he went, he'd gird his loins because all the old stories would come into play. That would make more sense to me because that's my routine. I noticed no one put in their online dating profile: hates family reunions. I guess that would make them sound too anti-social, honest, but anti-social all the same.

When a couple with wildly different personalities unites for good, it could mean they are a lot more alike than anyone suspected.

Changing Perceptions about
Hot Dogs and Dating

I PULLED OUT THE NEWSPAPER grocery flyer when I noticed ninety-seven percent fat-free beef hot dogs were on sale. I was excited because these dogs are almost entirely fat-free and only have forty calories each. Your average hot dog has two hundred calories or more. When I first tasted them, I didn't like them because they were different. The taste consisted solely of beef and a few spices. Reading the calorie content changed my perception entirely. I decided I could like them. My viewpoint changed about hot dogs. Oddly enough, my dating perceptions changed, too.

One of the first ones to fall by the side of the road concerned the never married guys. Early on, I thought guys who never married were a good bet. They didn't have an annoying ex, who either hounded him to do household duties at his former home or posted cryptic sayings on his Facebook page. He also didn't have children who made demands at odd times, often canceling any outings the two of us might have planned. Ironically, I thought of the bachelors as untouched by any woman. Let me clarify that, I don't mean sexually. Women put their stamp on men.

A man who has been married or in a long-term relationship will expect other women to act like the former females he's known. This is, of course, his perception of women. This also explains why a man out of a recent divorce, especially if stomped on in the proceedings, is down on womanhood. If his ex cheated, then he expects other women to cheat or eventually leave him for a younger, hotter man. Men milked like a Guernsey cow for financial reward expect future dates to act the same. So, you are dealing with all these divorced men expecting bad things because of their previous experiences. It makes the never married look tantalizing.

When you're in your twenties, a never married man looks like an appealing prospect. You don't expect him to be married. In the article, *"A Good Time to Move,"* he doesn't expect it either to the point of living at home, partying hard on the weekends, and shirking the responsibilities of adulthood for as long as possible. With young men's failure to grow up, there has been a parallel of college-educated women committing suicide stating the inability to find a companion for a reason. Surely, a thirty-something bachelor would be a better prospect, you would think. He might be, especially in all those Scandinavian countries where the men tend to grow up faster and act like adults. Often men, especially American men, find themselves in endless puberty, never growing into manhood. Each year a man remains single should tell you one glaring obvious fact. He wants to be single.

As women, we love our fairy tales. We want to believe the noble bachelor just hasn't found the right lady. We idealized him as if he is Father Stag in **Bambi**. Nature lovers know the stag never sticks around and raises the fawn. His sole purpose is to impregnate the doe, and then he is history. Maybe long time bachelors are more like the stag than I realized. If he is looking, he will find someone. Everyone can find someone. Often, we find the wrong someone because we have false perceptions about that person and end up divorcing when we realize our mistake.

Some women refuse to date divorced men because they see them as flawed. Some woman rejected them. The carefree bachelor seems to skip through life not taking on a wife, family, and associated responsibilities. Often, we view this as playboy behavior, which often it is. Consider that women rejected him, too. The mark isn't as visible as the divorced label. When you live alone, you are used to having everything your way.

Anyone forced to play with or eventually work with an only child knows it can be a trying experience. This individual usually believes everything should be his way. He will have a very difficult time with compromise. A never-married bachelor can be like that, especially depending on how old he is, always expecting his way. In a good relationship, you make compromises. The never married man never had to do this. Things have always been his way. Now, he may like the idea of a wife, regular sex, and possible hot meals, but he is unwilling to make space for her in his life.

In fact, I've found by stubbornly attempting to date never married men that they want all their routines and domicile not to change. The girlfriend or wife would be more like a housekeeper who visits and tidies up. Most women take one look at this and hit the road. I did.

To be fair, I would like to point out my perception of the never married man is not everyone's perception. My grandmother married my grandfather, a life-long bachelor at fifty. His reason for not being married was extreme shyness. Luckily, he met my grandmother who was not shy at all.

There are men who do not want to marry, ever. Of course, you have your closet gay guys, who attempt to play it straight. With all this in mind, maybe that divorced man doesn't look too bad. At least, he wanted a relationship and initiated it. It is all a matter of perception.

Are You a Drama Queen?

ARE YOU A DRAMA QUEEN? If you are, then you are one of the top things men hate about dating and women, in general. Oh no, you're not a drama queen, you rationalize, not like those annoying girls you went to high school, college, or even currently work with. I guess that depends on what you think a drama queen is. Men rate the drama on five factors.

Are you late for everything? The lack of promptness factor on the psychological level is an extreme demand for attention. You're never ready when he comes to pick you up or you fail to meet him at the appointed time. I am not talking about being five or ten minutes late now and then or even calling to say you're running late. The tardy woman causes the man to cool his heels and often miss reservations or opening credits of a movie. This constant lateness is a sign of a diva who wants to make an entrance. No one cares if you make a late entry. Your date does, but not for long since, he'll be dropping you soon.

Overreaction is the second aspect of a drama queen that drive men crazy, and not in a good way. This can range from complaining about the weather to the movie starting without you. Most of these things cannot be changed by acting put out and pouting like Daddy's spoiled little girl. Remember your date is not Daddy and even Daddy gets tired of his little princess's tantrums. I've seen women go into a major meltdown in public over a broken nail. This does not impress your date. A man likes a woman who can roll with the punches.

The third factor involves your man. If any of you remembered seeing **Ten Ways to Lose a Guy,** the heroine is cozied up to her date watching a movie, and she immediately questions what he's thinking about. He replied that he's watching the movie; therefore, he's thinking about nothing. She then goes on to tell him that he's thinking about his old girlfriend to his surprise. Of course, we know she's doing this type of behavior to try to lose the guy. The behavior of the woman interpreting what the man is thinking is more common than most women are willing to admit.

This behavior coupled with the hot and cold attitude is a relationship killer, too. That's when a woman is crazy about a guy one day, but the next she refuses his phone calls. I realize some dating manuals advise this type of behavior to make a man think you're a sought after commodity. In truth, they tend to think of you as a drama queen and not really worth the trouble.

Being mean to others is not appealing to men or women, but the drama queen loves to employ this technique to get more attention. She's always onstage performing, even if it is only for herself. One episode of **Hell Date** featured mean girl extraordinaire. She insulted everyone from the door attendant to the coat check girl. She also sent her expensive meal back several times, even demanding to see the chef to complain. Her mortified date apologized profusely to everyone she insulted. When the little person appeared dressed as a devil, her date was obviously relieved. The sad thing was even though his date's behavior was just an act, for most drama queens being mean to the help is the real deal.

Drama queens invent drama. They retell stories to make themselves the victim. They aren't above creating tales to tantalize their dates, even using illnesses, real or otherwise, for attention. This is such a mistake because men dislike dealing with sickness of any kind. Eventually, the date figures out he's been sold a bill of goods and wonders if anything she says is true. The woman spends so much time making herself sound exciting that she has little time to spend on her date. I bet you've gone out with men like that before. It wasn't a very pleasant experience, was it?

So think about it for a moment. Men crave calm, not drama. A survey solicited this information from men of different backgrounds and age groups. The most notable constant among all of them was that they were single; which means you might go out with one of them. Yes, they are judging you if you're on time, if you overreact to little things, put words in their mouths, go all hot and cold, and if you're mean to the help. You are judging them, too. It helps to know some of the things that are on the drama queen checklist to decide if you might be guilty of one or two.

Lucky Thirteen

WHY HAVEN'T YOU FOUND THE right match? Is it you? Why does the other person treat you so shabbily? Could be that you have poor self-confidence, and you pick people who reinforce that. Remember people will treat you the way you treat yourself. Then again, it just might be the numbers.

The magic number used to be seven. Peter Todd published an article in **Wired** magazine that explains statistical evidence that found people usually dated twelve different individuals before they met their perfect match. Remember this was an average, which meant some people had fewer relationships and some people had more. Jennifer Cruise has a character in one of her books wildly dating men to find the one. A spiteful co-worker told her the number was seven hundred. This depresses the character horribly because she met someone back at man number twenty-three that she really liked.

Of course, this relies on you believing that there is "the one" out there. If you go out with a person who ridicules anything you do, drop him or her. No one needs someone who is not supportive. That type of behavior will eat away at you like acid.

I love to read all those sentimental slideshows that come up on the net that details what characteristic a person loves about another. Men will say they love it when their wife talks in a cartoon voice, uses code words for sex, takes a long time to get ready, snorts when she laughs, etc. What? We all heard those things were wrong, maybe even took some heat for having a few of them ourselves. When someone really loves you, your quirks become endearing.

Some of you swept by relationship seven with no sign of a soulmate. Don't worry too much, since the new number is now Lucky Thirteen. Why the change? It might be because there are more people. Perhaps people date more. Relationships are not lasting, putting people back into the dating realm. The biggest new dating demographic is people in their fifties.

Why haven't you met the perfect person for you by fifty? Maybe the universe really wanted you to appreciate your soulmate by sending a few also-rans your way. When you find the right one, you will be extremely appreciative.

If you ever wonder why there are so few good marriages or relationships in your immediate world, or the larger world, it is due to a scarcity mindset. My best friend's parents never actually spoke to each other. They spoke through the children. I asked my friend why they were married at all. She told me her mother married her father because her grandmother warned her he might be the only man who would ask. She needed to grab him while she could.

Many men and women believe they won't find a mate and grab anyone who is willing to marry them, even when they know it is a mistake. Thirteen may seem high, but it might be because people have to work out issues about what they deserve and need to look past surface appearance to find the inner beauty.

I've done the online dating scene where men only want to date leggy blondes under thirty while the best fit might be a thirty-something redhead with an attitude. Women are guilty of specifying men only six foot and over, which is only thirteen percent of the male population. Consider that some of those extra tall guys are married, gay, or not interested in you, which means you wiped out any chance of finding Mr. Right by being super picky.

Often, people make outrageous lists of traits so they can insist there are no good prospects out there. As for thirteen relationships, you might meet him at three or twenty-three. Sometimes, unfortunately, we let the right one go because we are looking for this Prince Charming specimen. The sweet, nerdy guy who opened your car door wasn't it. Years later, you might realize he was, but now he's married to an infinitely smarter woman.

Is Love Dead on the Road?

EVER FEEL LIKE LOVE DIED somewhere? Maybe hit by a fast moving semi and splattered on some unnamed road. Sometimes, I feel that way. Other times, I wonder why love comes so quickly to others. That was the discussion when I saw my middle sister. We both are divorced and are always amazed that our older sister married a prince of a man when he was only the second person she dated. Over the years, we have discussed in detail why some women have all the luck to love and marry well. Here are a few possible answers.

TIMING

Our sister was in the right place at the right time to meet her husband. If she stayed home and bemoaned the lack of eligible men, she would have never met him. Let's face it, ladies, we have to be out doing things to meet people. Not counting Jehovah Witnesses and the guy selling Kirby Vacuums, no one comes to your door. Sometimes, your time is not the right time. Because you want someone right now doesn't mean the right man will come along when you want it, rather it is when you least expect it. Many couples, after they finally get together, find out they attended many of same events, even the same school or church without ever having met before.

BEING OPEN

I've talked before about being open to possibilities. Often we decide on a very narrow range of people we might actually accept as friends or lovers. Still, within that narrow range, we're not open. Are you making eye contact? Smiling? My oldest sister likes to retell the story of meeting her husband. She spotted him in a crowded college class that was putting her to sleep. The first thing she noticed, besides his curly afro, was the fact he seemed to understand what the prof was saying. When he turned and smiled at her, she smiled back. By being open, she soon found herself in a study group with this engaging man, even though he was nothing like her old boyfriend.

BE WILLING TO TRY AGAIN

I meet wonderful women all the time who confide they are unwilling to date again because they've been hurt. I understand. I guess it is all in what you want. Decide what you truly need. I need love and work. I've had some bad jobs, but I never thought to never work again. Working is essential to my life, so I went out and got another job. My goal was to get a job, not to hope to get close to getting one. There was no other option, but to get one. I believe you have to have the same approach to dating/love. You have to expect it will happen instead of counting all the reasons it won't happen for you. (I know this seems like a contradiction of earlier advice, but if you don't act like you're worthy of love, then you'll never find it. Love yourself first.)

My grandmother was not counting on love after surviving an arranged marriage. In fact, she didn't really believe in it. At the grand age of forty-seven, she met my grandfather and decided to try again. Of course, she could have decided to live alone.

STAND BY YOUR STANDARDS

My middle sister and I debated why we were divorced while our older sister was married and came up with a simple reason: we didn't pick well. I know a few cynical people might comment that we both must be difficult people. I beg to disagree, but will point out my elder sister can be difficult, and she's the one who is happily married. We didn't pick men that understood the complexities of marriage. As far as holding to a standard, I think we can both agree that we didn't have a standard...that's where our problem started. Know what you want, don't settle for anything less. I am in awe of the dating goddess who has dated one hundred fifty men in the United States and is expanding to overseas to meet her standard. (I feel obligated to add here...make sure your standard exists. My best friend's geeky brother is still holding out for a supermodel. I wonder if either of us should tell him she's not coming.)

PACKAGING

Okay, I know it shouldn't matter, but it does. Men like women who look feminine, not like one of the guys. Just yesterday, I was in the expensive part of town, but I had a shoe coupon for an exclusive shoe store. Naturally, I went to the store and scored a cute pair of flats on clearance. The one thing I couldn't help noticing on this warm, spring day was how dowdy the women were dressed. Most had on mom jeans or sweatpants combined with running shoes. Few men will look twice at that ensemble because it screams "not interested." I know some might argue that they weren't looking for a guy so they didn't dress the part. You don't know when you will bump into someone. Since I started my dating journey, I've run into men at the grocery, the dry cleaners, even the post office. Thinking back, the one thing all those encounters had in common was that I still had on my dressy work clothes. You don't have to dress like a fashion plate, just make the extra effort when you step out of the house. My daughter has turned into a fashionista and refuses to let me leave the house in athletic shoes unless I am going to the gym.

Dressing well has the added benefit of making you feel better about yourself. When you feel better, you'll smile more and men will perceive you as being more attractive and approachable. Anything feminine is a plus from a skirt to a colorful scarf. Be glad you're a woman and celebrate it. I was told by a man recently that a ponytail pulled through a baseball cap can be sexy, paired with well-fitted clothes of course.

LUCK

Don't discount luck. Why do some women marry their high school sweetheart and live happily ever after? It's not because they were more deserving than you. It was plain blind luck. How does your best friend meet the love of her life in another country when he was living just five miles away from her all his life? Luck again or maybe it's fate. How did my sister end up in the exact same class as her future husband? Maybe it was the only class offered at that time, or maybe it was luck again. The one thing I noticed about lucky people is they are always out trying new things when success happens. Good fortune does not come knocking when you're at home whining about your lack of it.

As for my luck, it is changing for the good. I've always been the same person, at times skinnier and younger, but the same. As for love, it is not dead on the road.

When He Doesn't Call

YOU MET A GREAT GUY. Perhaps you went out a few times. Maybe you thought something would really come out of this relationship, but then he doesn't call. First, it is a couple of days, a week, maybe even three weeks. It is clear he's not calling. Many women will immediately call him, an awkward conversation ensues, and then he immediately blocks her number.

It is possible he lost your number, but it is rather rare. Most men have the woman's number in their cell phone or it's attached to the email you sent him. He could have written it down somewhere on a calendar or a scrap of paper. Still, if you believe he lost it, or you feel like being pro-active, text him, don't call. If you call, you may slip into a whiny attitude and attack him for not calling. A text can be short, even flirty, but should never mention he didn't call. Instead, it reminds him there is a fun female out there he might want to see again. It also allows you to save face, too.

Why hasn't he called since you thought everything was working out so well? There is a chance he felt things were moving too fast. You made the mistake of calling him your boyfriend and mentioned introducing him to friends. You may have talked about the future. You know what I mean. Those questions about what type of house does he wants to live in, and what neighborhood, as in the two of you. Even men intent on marrying tend to get nervous when those questions come up.

Maybe you were feeling so close and personal that you confessed some intimate details. Could have been the tequila talking, but you still revealed you cheated on your last boyfriend. Your indiscretion could have been stealing from your company, or that you fake orgasms. Whatever it is, your current date didn't like it and has deleted your name from his phone. There really are no do-overs because it will stick in his mind.

Have you ever gone out with a guy, and the longer you dated him, the less you liked him? You come to the point where you decide never to see him again. Happens to men, too, but with technology being what it is they just cut all contact. He doesn't call, text, or email. This is his message that things aren't working out. You represent too many "can't tolerate" as opposed to "must haves" on his list of girlfriend qualities. He didn't know this initially but found out through various scenarios. One male co-worker informed me that women will keep up a façade for as long as ninety days, before exposing their real self. I noticed that was the length of most of his relationships.

He doesn't call because he is busy with an old girlfriend or ex-wife. Nothing makes a man look more delicious than being involved with another woman. Often it brings out the competitive spark. Some men decide to date to encourage jealousy. It doesn't matter who started the fire. All you need to know is they're having a bonfire, and you're not invited.

You may have read the signs wrong entirely. He may not even consider that you're dating. Do you only talk at work? Did you share a cup of coffee or a meal with other people? Did he ask for your number? Did you offer it without him asking? Many men will take your number with no intention of calling you. They think it is the polite thing to do. Some men will even ask for your digits as a way of ending the conversation with no desire to follow up with a call.

Then there is the guy who infrequently calls, maybe every two months. He's not a man who squires you around to the finer establishments. In fact, he's good with grabbing a pizza and hanging out at your house. You think you have a relationship because you share some sack time. You are a friend with benefits. As one of my high school students put it, an FWB is someone you wouldn't be seen in public with but puts out. How do you know if you're an FWB? Does he NOT introduce you to his friends or family? Are you NOT seen in public at high profile events? Does he call you sporadically and want to drop by? If so, then you are.

Then there is the guy who is already in a relationship. He flirts with you because it feeds his ego. Even though he took your number, he has no plans to call you. He could have bet his friends he could get five women's number before the night was over. In the end, if he did call, you'd probably become a friend with benefits. If you flatter yourself and declare you can take him away from his current girlfriend or wife, you'll end up with a man who will leave you eventually, too.

You met him. Both of you felt an incredible connection. You jumped into bed immediately. It was great, and yet no call. He has moved onto a new female. Men do not feel the same attachment after sex that women do. Often, they feel no attachment at all in early stages of dating. That's why he doesn't call.

In the end, if he doesn't call, move on. He is giving you a powerful message—the biggest one is that he's not that into you. The second message is he's just rude. If he ever does call, act confused. Make him repeat his name, then pause, as if thinking who he might be. A man can't pursue a woman who is chasing him. You have to decide if he is worth giving another chance. Keep in mind if he disappeared off the radar screen once, he could do it again.

Why Men and Women Can't Be Friends

AN EXPERIMENT TOOK EIGHTY-EIGHT male/female pairs of friends and invited them to a coffee experiment. The designers of the experiment did not want to risk any resulting data leaking out to the participants and destroying the friendships. With this in mind, the city where it took place remains anonymous, but the participants were English speakers. Are you aware in many non-English speaking countries the concept of platonic friendship between a man and a woman is laughable?

The couples drank coffee, and then separated for an interview supposedly about their beverage. The interviewer digressed into an offhand conversation about the friend. Questions revolved around regarding their friend's hotness factor, or if they would ever consider their friend in a romantic fashion. The females assured the interviewer their friendship was only platonic while the vast majority of guys were very interested in becoming romantic partners. The few who didn't confess to an attraction to their female friend may have just been lying because they felt the question was suspicious.

It is pretty much what every guy has ever told me, but I refused to believe. One male blogger grabbed this topic and told his tales of unrequited love where he stayed friends with a girl over thirty years in hopes he'd work his way into her bed. He did, after her last divorce, but then found he could no longer be friends with her. He has now entered **The Twilight Zone** of friendships. Things had been okay before they slept together. Truthfully, he was grooming her for romance. He had a goal, but once he reached it, he had nowhere else to go. The things he did that made him such an excellent friend from remembering her birthday to sending her positive messages when she was down, he no longer had any motivation to continue. Men are very goal driven. They are more about the hunt than the eventual catch. Some men are more like catch and release fishermen. The two drifted apart after a thirty-year long friendship.

Can men and women never be friends? All the movies, magazines, and trendy books tell us we can. Women can be friends with men they don't find sexually attractive. It is like having another girlfriend or a gay best friend. No man wants to know he's not attractive. His platonic friend will lie to him, and tell him he's attractive, which he translates to having a chance with her.

My sweetie assures me that men do not talk to women they aren't interested in. Even casual conversation with a stranger is a hook to reel the woman in. The man who settles for the friendship role is playing the long game. Women argue that they have great male co-workers or long time family friends. The male colleagues are people you have to work with, but it does not mean there may not be some underlying flirtation there. That's why people use the terms work husband, work wife, and emotional affair.

A woman who engaged in this discussion pointed out she had several male friends that she and her husband shared. What she really meant was they socialized with several couples. Usually, the women do something together while the men choose a different activity. Out of these long-term friendships, when the spouses die, it isn't uncommon for the friends to marry. Some might say they marry for companionship. Who's to say that the male friend wasn't looking for an opportunity, especially if his wife died first?

Ironically, women who treated their gay best friend like a girlfriend. Taking him everywhere, and even dressing in front of him, were surprised to learn he was sometimes open to taking a walk on the other side. Women adore the gay best friend because he brings in the girlfriend quotient without any of the competitiveness, while still bringing the male presence. Most women realize on some level that male/female friendships seldom work.

If this is truly the case, why do women offer friendship when they break up? Some believe they can be friends. Others like to keep the man on a string for backup purposes. Most feel guilty due to the breakup. They may occasionally comment on his status to maintain the conversation going but soon drift away with a new man. Defriending a man or deleting him from your cell phone seems so permanent and cruel, but it is the best thing you can do for both of you.

You won't really be friends. Instead, you'll be people who dated once. Your insistence to stay friends will keep all the broken dreams and hurt current by continuing to socialize. He won't be comfortable sitting across from the table with you and your new man. He'll compare himself to your date. He'll wonder what the two of you are like in bed over the appetizers. An intelligent man wouldn't agree to this travesty. Why put your "friend" through this.

If you have a trusted male friend, keep in mind he may not want to hear your relationship tales. Well, he might if they're bad. That way the two of you can gang up on your latest guy. Keep in mind; he may just have ulterior motives for disliking your most recent date.

The Elephant in the Room

SEX IS THE ELEPHANT IN the room that women of a certain age do not talk about. Sure, the thought is there, but unlike Carrie Bradshaw on **Sex and the City** we do not openly talk about it much. Too bad, we could learn so much from each other. The current belief for online daters is that sex should happen on the third date with the reason being you don't want to continue dating someone who is a dud in the sack.

Whoa, I don't feel like I even know anyone that well by date three let alone want to share my stretch marks with him. In fact, I don't want to reveal my stretch marks to anyone. There is another prevailing belief from the other side, which might be the female side, that to withstand the sexual pull as long as possible.

Men value what they have to work and wait for. Exactly what your mother and grandmother told you, but being a child of the seventies you rejected it. In both the books, **Dating Like a Man** and **Why Men Loves Bitches**, men polled about their reactions regarding sex laid it out plain. They will always take what they can get, but with women they waited for and developed a companionable relationship with resulted in better sex. It became an added bonus on top of a strong union. Women who are having sex on the second or third date end up throwing the man into a quandary. He gets what he wants, but may not even like the woman, then he doesn't know what to do. He may disappear off the radar screen or only shows up for booty calls.

Ever pick out a man you know would be perfect for you. He meets all your background criteria, and he's not too hard on the eyes. You know the two of you could make beautiful music together, but by date two he is showing some bizarre behaviors. Some of these things may not make an appearance until date six. It would be a shame if you made the mistake of jumping into bed with him. Once a woman sleeps with a man she feels obligated to stay with him. This is more than emotional.

During intercourse, a woman releases Oxytocin, a hormone that encourages bonding with her partner. That's why women want to cuddle after sex. Men don't experience this immediately that's why they can literally walk away and often do. In an established relationship, men can experience an Oxytocin release, but this takes both time and emotional attachment. Women often have sex to develop a relationship, but it doesn't work that way.

In this world, we still live by a double standard. Often, on dating profiles men will specify they want women with sexual experience, but in the end, they don't want to think you've slept with other men to get it. This tidbit defies logic. That's why the woman who jumps in bed with a guy early on kills the romance. He starts obsessing on all the other men she'd probably jumped in bed with on the third date and doesn't like feeling like one of the pack. Everyone wants to feel special.

The truth is he focuses on the chase. It is **Animal Planet** all over again. Watch a nature show where a cheetah is running down the gazelle. What happens when he catches the gazelle? The camera may cut to the horizon as the cheetahs munch away. Same with humans, once the chase is over, no matter how it ends, it's over.

While the chase is on you can show a man how you would like to be treated...with respect. You are a valuable commodity, a unique individual. I remember hearing a comedian say men used to talk about their woman's measurements with pride, but now they are thrilled to find a woman with a job and a benefits package. There is a great deal of truth to that. You have more to offer than you even know. Don't give it away. Men respect what they have to work for, but men can get into the habit of respecting and treasuring you. This was news to me, too!

This works only when a man pursues you and is unsure of you. The woman who gave it all up on the second date no longer gets royal treatment. Her guy drops by to eat food she's cooked and watch some television to be followed by some sack time. Some women call it a relationship. What does the woman really get out of that?

People forget the short-term items unless it goes into the long-term memory. An action or phrase has to be repeated at least SEVEN times before it will go into long-term memory. Other studies declare that it takes twenty-one days to develop a new habit and thirty days to break an old one. With this information in mind, do you think a man will be in the habit of treating you like the valuable individual you are in the course of three dates? Probably not.

Wouldn't it be great to have a man wait on you for a change? Women for so long have looked after their man and family, but who takes care of the woman? It has to be you. Don't sleep with men you don't want to have sex with—it's your right. You are never under any obligation no matter how much money he spends on a date. He had free choice to spend as much money as he wanted. Some relationships just don't have to go there. By dating, you may discover a friend as opposed to a lover. Set your own timetable, it takes multiple occasions to get to know people. Do you honestly want to sleep with a stranger? As for those other men in the past, forget about them. That was then. We're living in the now.

You may be able to work your way around the elephant sometimes, but other times you run right smack into it. People have a variety of opinions about a mature woman seeking out romance. When I was twenty the thought of a forty-something woman even considering sex disgusted me. Now that I am on the other side of the coin, I feel more alive than when I was twenty. In the end, it's your decision, not anyone else's.

Overlooked Men

DON'T YOU JUST HATE IT when someone stereotypes you? I used to be a pastor's wife and automatically pegged as straitlaced and no fun. People acted peculiarly around me, afraid to take a drink or tell a racy joke. They didn't allow themselves to act normal. I never got to know them, and they certainly never knew me.

Often, we overlook excellent men because we put them in a stereotype box. It's a box we don't find particularly appealing. One that doesn't fit. Engineers, for example, are deemed to be boring, picky, and nerdy. You imagine some guy with coke bottle glasses and a pocket protector.

In my family alone, I have many engineers who all happen to be male. They are tall, handsome men who can tell a joke and always open a door for a woman. They are intelligent, considerate men. They even dress well with a little help. That's why I wasn't put off by the idea of marrying an engineer, which turned out to be my smartest life choice yet.

Short guys are often overlooked. Having longer legs does not guarantee better manners or personality. The shorter man is well aware he is at a disadvantage and works harder to be charming. If you can accept that you might always be the same height or taller, then there is a world of guys waiting for you. Recently, while attending a concert at the racetrack, I watched fit, handsome jockeys flirt with taller, but very interested females. These men recognized romance could come in a taller package.

Shy men don't generally attract attention. They can be just as fine as a chatty Romeo, but they hang back, unsure of their reception. The truth is you may have to approach the shy guy. Do not assume he will be unreceptive. Sometimes it takes work to bring a reticent male out of his shell, but it is well worth it. A shy guy will be much more romantic than you ever dreamed. He has had plenty of time to think of romantic scenarios while working up his courage to ask a female out. He will also be much more loyal. This is a rare quality in an atmosphere filled with online cheating sites.

Women overlook bad dressers, too. Not all men have a sense of style. Color blindness is usually a male trait. Men also do not find fashion that necessary. Those who do value fashion highly will not value you. Most men would love some assistance in the wardrobe department. Be gentle at first or he will think you are rejecting everything about him.

Men outside your racial group could be your next best thing. This is tricky, though. You might love the guy, but find his cultural norms too restrictive. You may not know this from the onset but may have to rethink as the relationship develops. Men born in the United States will usually have the same cultural background as you. If you embrace his old world style of thinking, then you might end up treated like delicate crystal.

Chubby guys get the friend treatment. He's a great friend, but I can't see myself going out with him. Wow, this is an unbelievable waste of resources in a country known for its obesity. Ironically, chubby women don't want to be seen with hefty guys. People tend to think they take on the characteristics of whom they date. It doesn't work like that.

Ever have a much younger or older guy flirt with you?

At first, you might have wondered about their eyesight. Their vision was excellent, and so was their attitude. They saw you and liked what they saw. They didn't see any age barriers. I have friends who have married men much older and younger than they were. At first, they had doubts but overcame them as they fell in love with their future spouse.

There are men that could be perfect for you. Unfortunately, if you don't widen your horizons, you'll never meet them. There really is no reason for you to be alone unless that's what you want.

The Lure of Ex-boyfriends

MEN ARE CONTRARY. Nothing appeals more than a woman taken. Especially if that woman used to be theirs at one time. How many of you swore when you broke up with your guy that he would see you were the best thing out there. He'd regret leaving the best thing that ever happened to him. Maybe you even kept tabs on him to make sure whomever he was dating was so much worse than you. Then, out of the blue, he calls texts or emails you. Maybe he bumps into you at your favorite retail store. None of this is an accident by any means.

There is a chance he suddenly realized you were the best thing in his life. Not hardly, but what actually happened is his last girl dumped his butt, and he's out trolling. In his attempt to find a female to soothe his male ego, he goes back to all the women he's dated. It is an easier fix than totally starting new. He's assured that they liked him once. The man knows you, knows what you like, or how he hurt you. Never fear, he'll reach into his bag of tricks and offer you things he never gave you in the relationship. You wanted emotional closeness, he'll confess he did too, and now he's ready. Of course, what happens when you reveal you already have a honey?

The mention of a current honey may discourage some, but not all. For many the lure of competition only eggs them on to compete for a woman they did not want before. This is where the old boyfriend shines surprisingly, by bringing up revised old times. In his version, you did not call him every name in the book and curse the day he was born. His best bet is to tell you he's realized you are the woman for him. He then pulls out everything he wants to do for you. Not surprising, all his promises are things you wanted him to do, but he never delivered the first time around.

As women, we want to believe. We want to find that he's changed, that we are the best thing in his life, and that he will deliver on all the promises. Chekov in **Star Trek** used to quote an "alleged" Russian proverb, "Fool me once, shame on you. Fool me twice, shame on me." You're too smart to fall for this. If you're weak, taken in by his professionally whitened smile and well-rehearsed lines, pull in a girlfriend. She spent over two weeks propping you up after the breakup. She is so not willing to do it again.

What about your current honey? The guy who delivers on his promises and stands by your side? What about him? Some of you might quibble that he's okay, but you've become fascinated with the one who got away. He's a cobra that will bite you in the end. Part of your current allure is that you're taken.

Why would your ex treat you better now? By even entertaining the thought of seeing him, you've just proved you have no standards by crawling back to him. You've shown him you don't have much backbone and little intelligence. You also just gave him permission to treat you worse than he did before. Is that what you want?

Wait, you might insist, I am only talking to him. I have no plans to see him or drop my current guy. That's what your lips say while often even the act of contacting him to tell him you're taken is viewed as an invitation. Your ex-boyfriend does not want to be your friend. All those people who say they are friends with their exes, I wonder what their real intentions are. Often, a man likes to keep his options open and have the ability to hook up with an old girlfriend now and then. He continues this path open by contacting her occasionally via text, or a "like" on her Facebook status, even bumping into her at her favorite store. You wonder how many times he showed up there to make that happen. I'm not sure what a woman's intentions are since I've never had any desire to be friends with an ex. Get real here, you broke up under terrible circumstances. Every contact you have will remind you of those old wounds. Why torture yourself?

Why are you bothering to even give your ex the time of day? Often we reinvent memories. Maybe things weren't as bad as they seemed. Maybe you misread him or some other nonsense. You make up some lame story that you'd ridicule your friends for if they came up with it. About this time, someone needs to dope slap you and say, "What are you thinking?" Did you not notice the man by your side who adores you? Who, unlike your ex, is here for you? Why do women, and men, go chasing after bad news exes?

They believe the fantasy their ex spins for them. Some women claim they want closure. I always considered a breakup a very definite closure. Some women are just greedy and cruel. They are greedy because they can't seem to resist any man, even when they know it will end badly. Maybe that should be stupid instead of greedy. They are cruel to their current honey who they throw away in a hurry for a chance to chase a dream they'll never catch because it does not exist. Ironically, they are also cruel to themselves because they will find themselves back in the same emotional hole they'd managed to crawl out of before, with great assistance from their girlfriend. This time their girlfriends probably won't be so accommodating.

Potential

DO YOU OFTEN FALL FOR the first man who smiles at you? His most redeeming feature is that he shows interest in you, and that's a big factor. You look him over and decide he's good enough. That he has potential. Maybe you can shape him up or form him into someone you can live with or at least have a relationship with. Whoa, you are making mistake number one that most single women make. Choosing a man who *might* have potential. Rather like throwing an unknown seed in the ground and hoping for corn.

Would you have your tooth pulled by a man who, some-day, if he made all the right choices, might become a dentist? Of course not, you are asking someone to do a job he has no training or inclination toward doing. Often the only reason a guy comes on strong is because he has nothing to lose. It isn't because you're his lifelong love.

It is similar to picking up a shaggy mutt at the dog pound and declaring he has potential to be a purebred, championship Doberman. You can't change the dog's genetic makeup or physical form. Plenty of women have attempted to remake men's physical forms into something they found more pleasing. It may have been successful if that is what the man wanted and only needed encourage-ment or guidance to make it happen. Usually, it is unsuccessful.

How would you feel about your guy telling you to lose

weight? I used to manage a figure spa similar to **Curves**. Often men would come in and buy a membership for their girlfriend or wife. These same men would drive their lady to the place and sit in the car while she exercised. Because it was in a strip mall, it had a glass front so the men could make sure their women were working out. Almost all the clients lost weight, except those customers. I bet they ate a gallon of ice cream every night while their controlling mates slept due to feeling they weren't good enough.

Lori Gottlieb, the author of **Marry Him: The Case for Settling for Mr. Good Enough**, argues that too many women fantasize about Prince Charming coming to sweep them off their feet. While they wait and twiddle their thumbs, they allow perfectly acceptable men to pass on by. This is true for people who want that perfect, unobtainable man who does not exist anywhere, but I am not talking about him. I am talking about settling for a guy who is all wrong on so many levels, but you think he has potential. You have to believe it, or you would drop him like so many of your friends have already suggested.

What is wrong with dating a man with potential? That determines what you deem potential. Mark Twain, when complimented on his writing, deferred it by saying that many other associates had much more talent and potential than he did. They chose not to use it. The difference between them and Twain is that he actually worked and produced a product. People with potential often remain at the possibility stage and progress no further.

Men do not want to change. Our personalities are set by the time we're two. If you meet a party animal, and he's forty-two, there is no hope he'll want to join you in the silent reading program down at the library. He may do it once or twice to please you, but don't get your hopes up. It isn't as if they don't want to please you, but you are asking them to change who they are, and that's wrong, and well— impossible.

Here's the major danger of molding someone who has potential. You do not like who they are right now. Instead, you fall for who they can be. Disgust replaces hope when the man never fulfills his potential. The man may have already left before you became disgusted.

People are who they are. If he is a player, then he will remain a player no matter how much you love him. Keep in mind players know how to manipulate you with stories about their damaged childhood, or not being understood by women. He makes you think you're the only one who 'gets' him until he drops you like a hot potato.

So what is the answer? People date to discover one another. Okay, once you figured out the guy is not who you thought he was, or who you wanted, stop seeing him. Don't talk about his potential or scour your memory for something positive about him. Don't become one of those women who put up with his bad behavior because he might have a moment of goodness.

Do things that interest you because it is easier to fall for someone with similar interests. We talk about chemistry all the time, but it takes more than chemistry to make a relationship work. Think back to the inappropriate men, you may have found yourself attracted to; you had chemistry. You thought he had potential. He didn't or not the kind you wanted.

If you are looking for a thoughtful, kind fellow, make sure you are likewise. Opposites attract while those with similar interests and outlooks bond. Remember to look for who a man is, not who you think you can make him into.

Even though it seems like heresy on a dating blog; it is fine to be on your own instead of settling for men with "potential." As a veteran of dating and marrying men with potential that potential never pans out.

The Faith Factor

WHO HASN'T SEEN A MOVIE or television show where two people of different faiths fall in love? In a sitcom, this provides laughs by having the mother of the son faint, or the father of the woman grouse about her new boyfriend. Many religions forbid you associating with an unbeliever. So how does faith factor into dating and relationships?

I noticed online that many men and women are willing to date people of differing faiths than their own. If this weren't so, they would have relied on relatives and friends or even participated in an arranged marriage. One reason people check that "Any Faith" box on their profile is to put out a bigger net. They've seen the offerings at their church, synagogue, or temple, and the pickings are slim.

Let's face it; for the most part, we like to do things with another person, preferably a person who finds us attractive and interesting. Although, most people who check Any Faith rationalize that other faiths can't be that different. Besides, they just want a date, not a life-long union. So when do the deal breakers happen?

Keep in mind that whatever religious faith a person professes will seem right to them, no matter if you have doubts about it. There may be parts of the faith you can't swallow. Many religions emphasize the man must be in control because women are spiritually out of control creatures who need guidance. If your date suggests how you should dress or talk to suit his faith walk, remember this is only the beginning. It doesn't mean he's not a nice person, but he believes in his right to dominate you in all things. Will he change his ways for you? It is rather like asking a Dalmatian dog to turn itself into an Appaloosa horse. While they both have spots, they are two entirely different creatures.

On the other hand, people pretend to change to humor the other person even to the point of showing up at their church. If the relationship becomes serious, many devoted sweethearts will still expect you to convert before considering marriage. If you were only pretending to make him happy, are you willing to go through an entire life of play-acting? Perhaps you reason your faith isn't significant and you'd be willing trade it for a chance at this great guy. Should he expect you to throw it away just because he asked?

Truthfully, if someone respected you and your faith, then he would not ask you to do this. All honor in this relationship is deferred to the person's faith, as opposed to the mate. In some ways, this is just another form of witness dating where your date's end goal is your eternal salvation and conversion to their faith. Most likely, they aren't interested in continuing a relationship because there are so many other people to date and save.

What does respect look like? It is sometimes better describing what it isn't. Any attempt to ridicule your faith or prove why it is wrong is not respect. Your fellow sits on the couch and informs you that your Bible demands you should be submissive to your husband/man, so bring him another drink. Respect honors the other person's religious beliefs by allowing her or him to practice them freely. This doesn't mean you agree with them or even participate, but you value the person.

Spirituality is a private thing, but ironically, people tend to wave it like a flag or wear it as if it were the jersey of their favorite team. If faith is a cause of disagreement between the two of you, then it will be an on-going battle, even if it is unspoken. Thousands of people of different faiths date and even marry every day. How do they make it work?

They accept their beloved's faith as part of who they are. Often, the couple will attend different services. If this is an issue, then it is better to forgo this relationship, especially if you spend most of your time trying to explain to your sweetheart that he's hell bound. This is emotional abuse.

Sometimes people meet, become a couple, then one has a conversion experience substantially altering him or her. This changes everything. It is rather like your husband telling you he is going to become a woman. Even though you love him, you didn't sign up to marry a woman. Faith is a personal issue, but often it does affect your loved ones. Your sweetheart/husband's conversion may cause him to insist you must wear a headscarf or dresses that fall below your knee, or give up eating all meat or animal-based products. This is inherently wrong. It is not your faith. Why should you follow concepts you didn't embrace? You shouldn't, although some women will reason the preservation of the relationship remains paramount.

Dating someone of your faith is no guarantee of happiness. People of the same faith divorce every day. You can also date someone of a similar faith, but you have different degrees in your faith belief system. He might go to mass every day when you hit major holidays. So what is the answer, or is there even one?

The two of you met at church camp for middle-class

Protestant kids living in the Midwest. You both have similarities, besides your faith, that actually unite you. The more you share, the more successful your relationship will be. Unions based solely on religion usually aren't successful. (Sometimes, this is misleading because many faiths do not allow couples to divorce. A bitter, acrimonious marriage is not a desired pairing.) At the beginning of your mixed faith dating, your family or friends' disapproval gives you the spice of being romantic adventurers, but that wears off. What remains makes the difference. If you can't respect your companion's religion, then you can't respect him either. Who needs that?

Your Gaggle of Men

EVERYONE HAS HEARD IT TAKES a village to raise a child. Apparently, it takes a gaggle of men to keep a single woman happy and content. If so, what chance does one man have? I offer up two articles recently in the news. From CNN, Ian Kerner, a sexuality counselor offers up that a single woman does much better with a gaggle of men. This is based on a recent book called **The Gaggle** by Jessica Massa.

What does she mean by a gaggle? Your typical hot, single chick flirts with her male barista in the morning. She lunches with her male co-workers and has at least three boyfriends she dates in rotation, and another one basically in training. She Skypes her ex-boyfriend weekly, and then there's her butcher who's willing to do any type of particular cut for her at the grocery. This sounds like a script for a movie, not someone's life. If we did know someone like this, we'd probably call her names, because we're jealous, and doubt her commitment to any of the men.

We'd be right because Ian Kerner, the counselor, points out that she has to have this many men not to get drawn into a committed relationship. This keeps it fun. It is like being the Bachelorette, but it never ends. Does anybody believe the Bachelorette sleeps with three different guys in one week, then decides she is in love with one? No way. A relationship takes times to develop in isolation. We aren't who we really are when we are constantly in competition with a romantic rival. The man becomes Mr. Romance trying to outdo the other man. When a woman settles into a relationship or even marriage, she is disappointed that the man isn't the romantic superhero who had to compete with the gaggle.

The woman becomes restless and turns to Ashley Madison, a popular hookup site, for some action on the side. Ashley Madison is not for people who want to leave their current relationship, but more for people who want the romantic boyfriend and the husband, too. I am sure some people who sign up carry on multiple affairs. All participants are aware that they are engaging in an affair with married folks. There shouldn't be any of those **Fatal Attraction** deals where the woman tries to kill off her lover's family. However, there are no guarantees.

Interestingly enough, the profile for the Ashley Madison female cheater was a woman in her thirties, married less than five years, with one child. She is usually in the medical or education field. Now keep in mind, this woman hasn't been married all that long, but she is already considering stepping out. Another statistic that supports her behavior is there is less divorce in an economic recession because people just can't afford it. I've heard this from women who'd admitted they'd divorce their husband, but he makes good money. The solution is cheating, which put excitement in life that has become ORDINARY.

That's right, women chafe at going to work every day, coming home to the same person, doing chores, and paying bills. While dating a gaggle of men, the woman never cooks, forget grocery shopping, and she seldom cleans house. She counts herself lucky to get to work on time, and get her bills paid. She may have a few high earners in her gaggle that insist on picking up some of her bills to get the edge on their competition. A woman dating other men becomes more desirable than a woman dating one. It is the hunter instinct in the men. The woman's total efforts include slipping into sexy clothes to be wined and dined, and accept compliments and gifts. It all sounds good.

When she finds herself picking up her preschooler, going to the grocery, and finally arriving home to start dinner. The life she thought she wanted with the stick people on the back of the mini-van doesn't look so great anymore. Still, she wants it and her old dating life back, too. Many marriage therapists suggest a weekly date night to keep unions humming. What we really need is a mindset change?

As a consumer nation, we tend to think we can always get something new or better. Not true. Maybe the thought of having a gaggle of men appeals to you. How many men enjoy being part of a gaggle? Not many, according to surveys. Unless you're a player, and you had no intentions of ever having any type of relationship, then it's the gaggle for you. Remember our behavior changes with the relation-ship. Many people joke that once they settle into the relationship; they can wear their favorite T-shirts and sweats. You should be able to be real in your relationship, not punished when you are real by your spouse cheating on you.

Most people declare they want someone who "gets" them. You're never going to find that person as long as you're scrolling through all your possible gaggle members. No time to lay down roots to make an authentic relationship. It reminds me a little of **Multiplicity,** where Michael Keaton figured out how to clone himself. He made himself into a gaggle of men. One romanced his wife, another did home repairs, another went to work, etc. At first, he thought this was a great plan. He soon realized his clones were flat people since they only served one purpose. Makes you wonder if you have a gaggle how genuine are any of those relationships.

Reminds me of advice I once heard, that you never want to marry a player because he is used to a great deal of adulation, and one woman won't be enough. So if you got used to your gaggle, would you ever be content with one man? Good question, in Michael Keaton's case, his wife wanted him to be one person with different facets.

Greedy

REMEMBER THE OLD FEMINIST MANIFESTO that women could have it all, which at that time meant a husband, a clean house, well-behaved kids, and a high-powered job. It all sounded good, but few, if any, females ever had it all. It was just too much to expect. It didn't stop anyone from wanting it or even expecting it could happen. The same with dating, because we refuse to believe we can't have it all.

What does a woman want on a date or even from a prospective mate? Many men think she wants everything from a man who treats her like princess and is a high wage earner. Add to that a man so handsome that he is often mistaken for a movie star. Oh, and the woman wants constant excitement and novelty. He needs to surprise her with gifts, cards, flowers, and romantic getaways. There are no relaxed nights in sweats watching a DVD for him.

Sounds like a bit much, surely the sources jest. I am not sure, but that is the message they got when their girlfriend or wife left them for someone they believed could meet all these wants. I have serious doubts anyone could do it all, and if he could, then he could not do it all for long. That is what they refer to in marriages as the honeymoon period. When all the newness wears off and just everyday life remains, some couples grow indifferent and drift apart. Bored with their situation until someone new and shiny comes along sparking their interest, and the cycle begins once again.

We, as Americans, are greedy. We even have a television show called **American Greed** dedicated to telling us about all the devious things people will do to get more stuff. Same with relationships, we'll do a lot to hook the man even pretending to be what we aren't. This is one reason Fredericks of Hollywood makes so much money. Women are willing to strap on fake boobs and butts, and wear outlandish wigs to attract a guy. Maybe even pretend an interest in a sport they do not like. Women do all sorts of things to land a man and not like what they landed. Number one because he prefers a curvy, blonde-haired woman who know football. Number two, he was probably playing fast and loose with the truth, too, and he's not the romantic hero he pretended to be.

Is it perception or greed? It is a little bit of both. The media tells us we can have everything, We deserve it. We're worth it. We hear it over and over again. We are told nothing about setting priorities, what matters most in a relationship, and how to judge character. We assume things that aren't true and often give a handsome man the benefit of the doubt while the average guy gets no benefit at all.

Men were asked, if, in the end, they preferred a woman with some weight on her who would treat him well or a skinny chick who would be mean to him. The majority picked the first. So knowing this, you'd think women might work on their kindness ratio as opposed to the treadmill, but you'd be wrong.

Despite a mountain of evidence, people still expect to find that perfect person out there somewhere. They leave wonderful, caring people to chase after a mirage. An illusion inspired by glitzy, Hollywood movies, glossy magazines, and even books. People are simply imperfect creatures doing the best they can. Why would anyone be perfect in every way? If they were, then why would they want you?

I think it comes down to greed. We expect the best of everything with doing nothing to earn or deserve it. Then the woman, and sometimes the man is angry when that perfect mate doesn't come along. They'll chase after people they believe to be perfect, discarding them when they find they aren't. They'll try to shape people into the image they want and become embittered when their creations desert them. If they're lucky, very lucky, then they'll grow up and realize the world doesn't revolve around them. Once that epiphany happens, they'll notice their imperfections and humbled by the realization. Next time around, they'll try to be a better person aware that a relationship involves two people.

Amazingly, once they realize they do not deserve a perfect person they will become the perfect match for someone who thinks likewise.

Dating and Texting

YOUR TEXTING MAY BE THE symbol of where your relationship is at and where it is going. I overheard two women discussing the gradual disintegration of one woman's last romance. At first, she talked to her man every night, the calls grew less frequent, he started texting her, then even the texts became shorter and were often abbreviations that never spelled out 'I love you'. The sympathetic girlfriend asked her friend when she knew the relationship was doomed.

Men, pay attention to the following sentences, because her answer is relevant, and I will explain why in a second. She replied without any hesitation. She knew the relationship had turned the corner when he started texting.

There are times it is ok to text, but not as many times as you think. If you are running late, you might text that you are late. Texting generally implies you don't care enough to call. If you are crazy about a person, you want to hear his or her voice. You text if you are keeping her on a string with a bunch of other women. You text when you are hanging out with the guys, and you don't want to interrupt your male bonding to talk to her, even though you said you'd call. You text when you are watching your favorite television show. What all these things have in common is that you consider them more important than the actual woman. You text when you are on a date with another woman. You text when you are drunk. Trust me; she knows all these reasons.

Teenagers might build a relationship with text messages, but grown women want face time. If they can't have face time, voice time will do. Bad things happen with texting. Your friends think it is cool to text for you. A message goes to the wrong person. A sarcastic or funny message comes off wrong. Women, unfortunately, get rotten messages via text from breakups to date cancelations. Just ask any woman whose ex-husband notified her via text that he wanted a divorce. Sometimes the idea of a text message has negative connotations.

Are you serious about this woman? Then keep the texting at a minimum. Michael Masters, author of **TextAppeal—For Guys! The Ultimate Texting Guide**, states that the hotter a woman is, the less texting you should do. Unnecessary texting makes you look needy. Inappropriate texting such as in the early morning, late evening, even at work can be annoying.

You don't get to know someone through texting. There are no social cues to let you know you've entered into the boring zone. You can't really show off your clever wit or charm in a text. You may think you can, but typing ROFL doesn't quite do it.

Text messages sometimes function as smoke screens, allowing the man to hide behind them. Some men will be guilty of using the same message repeatedly on different women. Does it sound familiar like a song or poem? Then it probably is. Women don't want perfection. They just want to get to know you.

Another thing, as a female, I absolutely hate are men who text me and actually think I know who it is. No, I was not waiting for his text. The man is so unimportant in my life he isn't in my caller identification yet. Don't play a cutesy game about your identity, either. Always assume the woman doesn't know who it is.

When is it okay to text? Running late, confirming reservations, seeing if she got home safe, double checking preferences, to see if she's free to talk. Most women won't mind an occasional random compliment text or an 'I love you' text. In the end, they really want to speak to you. It doesn't have to be a long conversation. It is enough to make the effort, which will show her how much you care.

Never, ever text on a date. If you have to take a call or text, excuse yourself to do so.

Why Are Men Such Jerks?

WHAT SINGLE WOMAN HASN'T COMPLAINED about the men she's dated being jerks? A simple translation is she is not into them or they aren't into her. It could be they are jerks. Better yet, they are trying to act like idiots and succeeding. Would you believe they are reading advice on dating sites that are advising them to act in such an offensive way? Most men who are on the dating scene feel who they are and what they have to offer isn't enough. They either have been told such nonsense by an ex who left or rationalized it because they are currently single.

In their desperation, they searched the Internet for help. What better place than a dating website? Wouldn't the dating service want a person to hook up and live happily ever after? Not really. It is more like gambling. They have to have a few success stories to keep people trying, but if all single people got hitched after laying down their initial fee, then they'd be out of business.

In an article posted on Match.com's website, one of the things a man is told is to talk about himself, as opposed to showing interest in his date. I've been out on a few of those dates. A man who talks about all the wonderful things he's done in his life. Anyone in sales knows the customer (the date) is interested in how the merchandise (you) will enhance her life. To demonstrate this, you must find out what she likes. To make a sale, you show interest in her life which translates into her feeling good about you and whatever you're selling. A man who talks about himself is considered an egomaniac. You can also look forward to more of the same on future dates. There is something to be said about holding back. What is left to be discovered if a man blurts out the details of his life on the first date?

If oversharing didn't win your heart, then the man should insult and tease you. This almost sounds like advice you'd give to someone you didn't like. Remember how hard you worked to get ready for the date? How nervous you were about your appearance? How great are you going to feel about a guy who insults your outfit, hair, or shoes? He isn't going to be at the top of your list of guys you want to date. Maybe you almost tripped walking out of the restaurant, and for the duration of the night, he teases you about being clumsy. Probably feels a lot like being out with your annoying, younger brother.

What do you expect a man to do to make a good impression? Usually, they show interest in you, have excellent manners, and compliment you. Men are urged to skip the compliments or go light on them. I am convinced my ex-husband took this advice. I resented the lack of compliments very much. Women, in general, do not get as much positive feedback as men, which translates into the need for some significant compliments. If you talk positive about someone, then you feel more confident about the person. So not only is your date robbing you of the warm fuzzy feeling a compliment would engender, but he is also robbing himself.

So far ladies, are you impressed? Next on the list is not to plan elaborate dates, just meet for coffee. This works for a guy because he doesn't have to spend too much time or money on you in case he views you as a dud. That is the feeling you'll get, too. Face it; sitting around in a noisy coffee shop is awkward. You need to be doing something, and it doesn't have to cost a ton of money, either. Avoid the man like the plague who just wants to hang. He shows an incredible lack of initiative and interest. A guy can plan a date that has stages. If meeting at a nearby restaurant for drinks works out well, then he can move on to suggest playing miniature golf later.

Rushing the relationship is another thing to avoid on the list. I guess that it is up to you what is rushing the relationship. There are guys who want to call or text you immediately after the first date, every day, even several times a day. Not normal. On the other hand, guys are often advised to play it cool; act like the bad boy who has several women on the line. After a week or more, he suddenly locates your number. I remember being treated like this, and I didn't like it. I didn't go out with the guy again. I distinctly remember him blubbering into the phone that he did like me. Could have. Who knows? This is one girl who didn't fall for the bad boys moves.

Let's look at this as if you were talking to a girlfriend. She tells you she recently went out on her second date with a man who monopolized the conversation. He also insulted her brand new shoes she bought for the date, instead of complimenting her. To make things worse, he thought it was cool to tease her about having braces at her age. Even though it was their second date, they were still meeting at Starbucks. She waited over two weeks for him to suggest a second date. What advice would you give her? Better yet, what woman puts up with this type of treatment? Remember if you do, you'll get more of the same and worse.

If you think your date is trying to act like a bad boy,

make a bold move and ask him to be himself. You might discover you like the authentic him better. That will be a good deal for both of you.

Are We Programmed to Pick Mr. Wrong?

THE OTHER DAY I WAS talking with a woman who claimed she was envious of me because my husband and I were taking off to celebrate our first anniversary. She confided that she and her husband never do anything special to celebrate. She admitted she'd hoped the second marriage would be better than the first, but it wasn't. My friend is an intelligent, likable, attractive woman. Why did she end up with a man who virtually ignores her? Women, anxious to escape a marriage or mate, whose relationship didn't turn out to be what they first thought it would be, initiate over seventy percent of divorces.

On the same day, I read an article on **Live Science** that explained our hormones make us go for the sexy, rule breaker when we are ovulating. At one time, the muscular male might have been able to run down a mastodon, but now he only hunts hot women. A thinking woman knows a dependable engineer would be a much better father and husband than the rodeo bull rider. Yes, but what does intelligence have to do with sex appeal? Naturally, very little, since women, even those who confess to wanting to get married, have negligible interest in men when they aren't ovulating. They may enjoy the idea of men, weddings, and the ivy-covered cottage, but not the actual male so much.

When women are ovulating, they want a he-man male

with a deep voice and wide shoulders, and buckets of testosterone. In the back of **Popular Science** magazine, there is a pheromone-based cologne average guys can buy to attract women like a bad boy. "The Scent of a Man" article stated that when women sniff T-shirts worn by men. The men with more he-man characteristics received many more thumbs up from the female participants. Why do women choose taller, muscular men with more defined male characteristics?

It is two-fold. In primitive times, the bigger, stronger man would pass on his dominant characteristics to the offspring and be a good provider. Keep in mind, in earlier times, the alpha male had several partners. Marriage didn't stop most men from having a mistress, girlfriends, or the occasional fling. Bad boys haven't changed over the years; it is the wives or girlfriends' protests that have become louder over the last fifty years.

Now women, even those non-ovulating females, go for the sexy, tall man every time, well almost every time. Why is that? The instinctual response may cause women to pick the most masculine sire for her children. What happens when a woman isn't ovulating? Why does she go for the same bad boy? Even to the point of dumping her dependable husband or boyfriend.

Media myths and internal lies are the reason. Every romantic comedy and many romance novels feature bad boys who tantalize the heroine with their charisma. After several grand gestures, he realizes he's in love, and then makes the ultimate grand gesture devoting himself to the heroine. It wouldn't be a sacrifice unless he had women chasing him. All the females in the audience sigh and press their hand to their heart, hoping they can meet such a guy. Often, women know they are being played but will suspend knowledge so they can hold onto the bad boy. Of course, they are holding onto nothing since he is doing what he does best, wowing other women.

Media informs us that the bad boys will be super romantic, whisking us off to exotic locales, wining and dining us, bringing us flowers and extravagant gifts. Some bad boys might because it is part of their shtick. Most won't, because they do not have to do anything but be a bad boy to get the woman. They do not have to be thoughtful or dependable. Often, they will stand women up, but the women are still eager to go out with them. The women believed they had reached some sort of status among other bad boy-loving women.

Often women marry the bad boy they fell for in the wedding of their dreams. The romance was great, but the happily ever after isn't happening. I am not saying that bad boys don't want to marry, many do, but they cannot change overnight and usually don't change at all. All those bad boy characteristics that drew the women in are also the predictors of him straying. The life the wife imagined never happens.

There comes a time when your bad boy ages out of the pheromone rodeo. In the animal world, there are almost no old alpha males because the younger men kill them. There are few things sadder than a middle-aged man trolling the bars using tired pickup lines that used to work. You probably can lasso a bad boy then, since his best days are long behind him. What do you get besides an embittered man who resents you since you now represent the best he can do.

Smarter women go for the beta male who's not second best. Instead of being a strutting peacock, he uses imagination and thoughtfulness to meet his woman's needs. Interestingly, the higher a man's intelligence and education, the less likely he is to cheat. Here's a guy who has figured out a one-night fling with a girl he met in a bar isn't worth tossing out a twenty-year marriage. Not so with the bad boy, another day, another woman, remember that next time you consider taking Too Handsome to be True home with you.

Ten Things Men Find Unattractive

I WILL ADD A DISCLAIMER that not all men find all ten things to be unattractive, but enough do to make it generalized list.

1. The angry woman. She is constantly in a rant about something. No one can do anything to her satisfaction, not the mail carrier, the server, and especially not her man.

2. Bad hair. This surprises me, but why should it? Statistics lists hair at seventy-eight percent as the thing a man notices first. Unfortunately, your hair could prevent you from getting dates. I am a professional, but I am shocked how often my fellow female co-workers sport greasy, flat hair. They rationalize it is only work. Datable men show up at work and at the places you stop at on your way home.

3. Being too anxious for a man. You know the woman she's like an obsessed hunter. She might even change into her hooker dress at work to make it to happy hour at the local bars. The fact she is hanging out on a bar stool alone in her five-inch heels, giving the death stare, to every beautiful girl in the place says it all.

4. Lack of personal grooming. Many men struggled with their visible reaction in the summer time when their date raised her arm only to reveal a hairy pit jungle. Other women choose not to shave their legs, because it's so

much work, and men don't notice. They do. In the United States, men expect a woman to be free of body hair, even down there.

There is a scene in **The Sex and the City** movie where the girls fly to Mexico. They tease the Miranda because she has hair coming out of her swimsuit. They imply no man would want to get close to that mess.

5. Clothes. Women come in all different sizes and shapes, but there are clothes that will flatter each figure type. Sloppy, dirty, unkempt clothes were major offenders, according to guys. Too tight clothes aren't flattering, either. They just make you look fat, which probably wasn't the plan. Don't dress like a man, unless you are hoping to attract a woman. Attractive, feminine clothing that flatters your figure is always inviting.

6. Unkempt hands and feet. There is a reason behind a nail salon on every block. Yet, women still show up on dates, even weddings, with nasty nails.

7. The Princess. She believes she is honoring the man by going out with him. She tells him what restaurant she wants to go to, theater performances, flowers, etc. She expects everyone to bow and scrape to her, too. It is embarrassing to be seen with this woman, because she is so hard on everyone, especially her date. These women think it is beneath them to stand in line at clubs. The princess announces her opinion to the public so they can have as high of an opinion of her as she does.

8. Curses like a sailor. An occasional swear word might slip out of a woman's mouth when tackled by a mugger or almost hit by a semi. That's to be expected. The woman who has a larger collection of curse words than the aver-

age Marine, and isn't afraid to use them, is offensive. If a man wanted to hang with the guys, he could go to the sports bar to hear foul language. Keep in mind, a man might be shopping for a forever girl. A woman who keeps dropping the f-bomb is not a great prospect. I know it is a double standard, but I am giving you the man's point of view.

9. Promiscuity. This used to mean just flirting with other guys while dating someone else, not anymore. These are women who will engage in a fling with the FedEx man if they can but still keep their regular guy on the side. There seems to be no age range on this, either. An older co-worker had two men on the side while she lived with the third. Men don't like this. Think how you'd feel if you were part of a harem of women competing for one man's attention?

10. Posture. Never in a million years, would I have picked this one, but think about it. Models and movie stars don't stride around with slouched shoulders. Instead, their shoulders are back and head up as they confidently stride into the room at least for public appearances. Standing up straight makes you look five to ten pounds slimmer. I am able to lose my gut by standing up straight. Another reason to straighten up.

Niceness Is Always Appreciated

I RECENTLY READ AN ARTICLE on CNN website by Ronni Berke about the "Do's and Don'ts of Dating After 50." Here's a woman who ought to know. She's over fifty and out there, hoping to meet husband number three or at least a companion. What did I learn from the article? Actually, a great deal, but probably not what I was supposed to learn. I read dozens of comments that were very revealing about dating among the middle-aged.

Miss Berke had good advice on posting current photos, dressing appropriately, and working at being personable. A much braver woman than myself, she tried speed dating and was not impressed. The men were often nervous, rambled on about themselves, and one actually took her drink when he left.

The problem with speed dating is you expect people to do well in a nerve-wracking exercise. Instead of facing one woman's disdain, a man can experience rejection multiplied by twenty-two. Then there is the issue that the man talked about himself. Wow, this is difficult because books and Internet articles do emphasize talking about yourself so your companion can judge if you're the right type. I'll agree there comes a point when you speak about yourself too much, but in speed dating, you only have a couple minutes to present yourself. You are selling yourself to a potential buyer. Who is good at that? Salespeople, you've been sold plenty of things you did not want or need. Makes you think twice about Mr. Smooth.

Miss Berke complained that the men appeared nervous which didn't do anything for her. If a man wasn't nervous, then the implications are he does this all the time. It is no big deal to him because he gets women left and right. The nervous guy is the shy fellow, the hard working engineer, or the single father who has forced himself into this travesty in hopes of meeting a like-minded female. The guy, who is scared to death he'll say the wrong thing, is actually the man who cares.

Miss Berke took us down memory lane by taking us on her first online date. She gussied up and made herself presentable, but it was obvious by her date's reaction that he was disappointed. She vowed to arrive early in the future to check out her date first. I am not sure what her plans were, but many men and women arrive early only to preview their dates and leave out the back way if they aren't impressed with what they see. This is just mean and wrong.

The commenters, for the most part, took off the gloves. One middle-aged man admitted he carried more weight than he liked, but the rude reaction of women he tried to date floored him. They were willing to tell him that he was unacceptable and too fat to date them. Now there is no reason they should go out with him if they didn't want to, but there had to be a better way to say it. On the other hand, don't judge people totally on their physical appearance. Our appearances keep changing, especially if you've already hit fifty.

Too often, we base the whole dating game on looks, and that is such a small part. What is worse is putting your wrong foot forward before you even meet by posting old pictures. If you post a photo of when you were thirty and fitter, your date will be the type who wants a fit, thirty-year-old. Sure, you won't get as many replies with a recent photo, but they will be people who want to date you. Isn't that what you want?

Men and women on the dating scene are hoping to meet a companion. It could be short term or for life. With this in mind, a guy who doesn't spark your fancy will not want to be your friend. Ladies tend to think neutral dates could fill in until they find the right guy. Wrong. This only wastes the man's time and money. When he is out with you, other women see him as not available. This is a major reason men do not want to be your friend.

One of the commenters talked about how self-absorbed American women are. He advised that men should buy themselves a foreign bride. Good luck with that because it is often a scam or a free trip to the US. One man's potential wife took him for almost $800,000. He flew to see her several times, adding to the bill, but she never made it to the United States. She was too busy working on her singing career and living with her young boyfriend. I do know actual men who felt too inept to romance a woman, so they bought one, flew her over, only to be rejected when she arrived. There aren't any guarantees even with women you purchase.

What is the deal? Is there an incredible secret to dating in the middle years? I think being nice is it. Yes, just being nice. Treat people the way you want to be treated. Do you want your date to look bored while he plays with his cell phone? Probably not, so you shouldn't. Keep in mind, your date is trying hard and does not have James Bond charm to impress you. Ladies, men that wow you from the get-go are usually not men looking for a life companion. All they need to do is get you out of your stilettos for the night.

Which brings me to a crucial factor in dating, especially first dates, or speed dating. Watch what you wear. Sure, you want to be attractive and not fade into the woodwork, but an expansive show of cleavage or age-inappropriate clothes is just pathetic. Of course, your date gets a sexual miscue that you are offering. For the men, please dress up. Maybe not a suit, but a tie would be appreciated. All men look better well groomed. It also signifies you want to impress her. I haven't met a woman yet who wants her date not to care about his appearance.

The rules aren't that different for the over-fifty set. Please be kind. It costs you nothing, and it will change your life and someone else's for the better.

Rejected

HAS YOUR ONLINE ROMEO REFUSED YOU? Wonder why a person who you've never even met, let alone talked to, rejected you via online dating? Welcome to the weird and wonderful world of online dating. Before you become too excitable in your dislike, remember your luck in the dark bar atmosphere where you shouted over the music. There was the hiking club, the astronomy group, and the singles travel cruise all guaranteed to help you meet a possible mate. They were all good things. You may have met a few people you thought had possibilities until you found out they didn't.

What's with online date rejection before you even meet? Aren't online daters desperate, lonely losers, and online dating is their last chance? Well, you'd be wrong if you thought that. If you were under the impression, the people whose profiles you received would be extremely lucky to go out with you because they couldn't do any better, then you'd be wrong again.

John M Grohol, PSYD, author of "Who Uses Internet Dating" discovered that online clientele tends to be more social than previously thought. Consider how much courage it takes to meet new people night after night. The average age of an online dater is forty-eight, plenty of time to develop social skills. The Match and eHarmony users usually have high self-esteem and consider a romantic relationship an important part of their life. A person with low esteem won't participate in online dating or discontinues after one or two rejections.

Why do potential dates never respond to your initial inquiry? This is the main complaint from folks who purchased online dating services. They might be flooded with dozens of profiles, but few actually answer questions. One reason is their account isn't active. All dating sites keep inactive members to plump up membership numbers. They also do it to encourage the inactive members back. The inactive member gets an email occasionally that twenty women are interested in him. It works many times, but usually if the person is in a relationship, he ignores the message.

If the account is active, and the intended person does get your wink or questions then why doesn't he or she answer? Match.com did a survey to come up with answers. Many men complained of bad teeth, hair, and grammar. There is probably not a lot you are going to do about your teeth unless you whiten them. Men, even back 150 years ago, considered the lack of abundant hair reason not to marry a woman. Men still prefer women with long hair. They settle for clean, styled, and colored locks. Men do not want to date women with gray hair because it makes them look old.

As for your grammar, take time when writing your profile and emails to get it right. The man may not be looking for an English teacher, but he wants to feel that he is important enough that you will take the time to draft a decent response. Wouldn't you do this for the love of your life?

Debt is another tricky issue. Both sexes refuse to consider relationships with people who have over $5000 in debt or major school loans. The result is if things work out, then his debt will be your debt. It is best not to get started if the person has overwhelming debt. How this is found out before dating boggles the mind.

Distance is an issue for both men and women. Three hours seems to be the limit. Employed people do not have time to drive six hours round trip, so after they Mapquest a distance, and find it is too far away, they may just delete your profile. It is hard to know when people don't tell you.

Your photos might be turning people off and not for the usual reasons. If you are holding onto a drink or a beer bottle in any of the pictures, people assume you are an alcoholic. Women tend to think this more than men. If you're a woman and you're shown drinking, then it is assumed you are a party girl who will be out every night. The quiet astronomer or high earning engineer will delete your profile immediately. Some people do not get the courtesy of a hello because they are too good looking. Yes, you heard me right. Too good looking is now a pitfall. People assume you will be a cheater. If you sexed up the pictures with bikini or cleavage shots, then that shows your cheating nature, too.

Ironically, in the same Match survey, "Why People Reject Dates," being a virgin is a liability, too. With the average age forty-eight, it makes sense. More women than men found low sex drive and poor bed performance as deal breakers. This explains some of those stilted leading questions.

Often after the initial date, the person refuses to respond or agree to a second date. What went wrong? A whopping sixty-seven percent of online daters named poor hygiene as a date stopper. Interestingly, the second deal breaker was laziness. If the man or woman thought their partner was lazy, then they would refuse to pursue a relationship.

These are some of the top reasons a person might ignore

you. Unfortunately, the online dating formats no longer support a way to respond why you choose not to respond to someone. It could be a variety of things from developing a relationship with someone else, to not being interested in a relationship at this time, or even resemblance to an ex. In the end, you probably can do nothing since you don't know, but it might be wise to check your grammar, hygiene, and profile photos.

Why Women Dump Good Men

IT'S TIME FOR MY MASSAGE. My masseuse is an upbeat, attractive guy who is superb with his hands, and often chatty. He envies my relationship with my sweetie because he hasn't had any luck. His last four girlfriends dumped him, he confessed, but they cheated on him first with some bad boy type.

"Really, you're kidding me," I exclaimed from my prone position on the table. "You're a nice guy," I mumbled through the face rest.

I know he's a nice guy because of how he is with his own children and even his ex-girlfriend's children. He often plans romantic getaways for his girlfriend of the moment. Here is a thoughtful man who's willing to date women with children, and yet he seems to get dumped all the time. What gives? Why do women drop him? He wanted a list so I scoured my brain for what I knew.

Some women dump guys who do too much. They give too much early on proving they're needy, not a delicious prize like the tantalizing bad boy who gives nothing. Why do pickup artists get girls by insulting them or flirting with their girlfriends? Women tend to want what they don't have or seems hard to get. The guy who is too nice in the beginning doesn't look to be a prize. (I do want to point out the guy that seems like a jerk at the get-go is a jerk.) Women who enjoy this type of male behavior have inferior self-esteem.

Another reason a woman moves on is the appeal of variety. She may have a perfect guy, but is convinced another prize is around the corner. This is the female version of the player. Often, she overestimates her charms and believes she can play this game forever.

The flipside of this is the woman who married her first boyfriend who may be the real deal. He might be the best she'll ever meet, still she feels cheated. A steady diet of her friends' chatter, coupled with romantic comedies, makes her wonder if she made the right choice. Given a few years and a couple different guys, she may have done the same thing, but she doesn't know this yet. Instead, she chucks her faithful man in search of the paragon she believes is out there.

Women dump men out of boredom. We accuse men of this all the time and are surprised women are guilty, too. Women like more variety in everything from food to sexual positions. Many males are steak and potatoes men, meaning they could do the same thing repeatedly and be content. Women stuck in these relationships don't know how to introduce something new or have been rebuffed when they tried. Starting over feels more comfortable.

Women dump men who don't give them what they want financially. This isn't necessarily exotic trips and plastic surgery, but some women are accustomed to a very expensive lifestyle.

Ever know a woman who likes drama, chaos, and attention in her life. Then she won't be content with one guy. She'll start something with one, move to another while she is still dating the first one. That makes for plenty of drama. One man can never be enough for her. It isn't the sex either because most of the attention she is getting is from her girlfriends.

I hesitate to say this, but some women dump men that don't have the right look. Of course, you might wonder why they went out with them in the first place, but people change, along with their professions. Many nurses put their medical student husbands through school only to be kicked to the curb when he reached doctor status. Same deal with women who find their blue-collar boyfriend no longer suits their professional image. Maybe the man grew comfortable in the relationship and put on weight or wore sweats in public one too many times. Yep, women, discard guys who don't suit them rather like an out of season purse.

Do you have a friend who dates lots of men? She may have thrown away several nice men. The problem is she doesn't know what she wants. She thinks she'll find it by dating, but that doesn't work. She has to sit down, not for a few minutes, but often months to discover what she really needs and wants in a partner. How can you know if you have it when you don't know what you need?

Ever wonder why some elderly ladies are so crotchety? They've gotten to the end of their lives never living the life they wanted. They could have stopped at any time and made adjustments. They could probably throw out several reasons why they didn't do that. If you want something bad, you make it happen as opposed to going through life haphazardly.

Now, there are plenty of reasons to leave a guy, including abuse. The important thing is to leave as opposed to going out and cheating on him. Why do women do this? Some believe it is their right. Others think they won't get caught and they can have the man who is paying the bills and the bad boy. Often the woman wants to break up, and cheating seems to be the deal breaker that will make it happen. Still, other women are just trying out the merchandise before deciding which one she wants.

Women often believe men don't take romantic breakups hard. They do. They take them very hard. Surf over to a website called Men Going Their Own Way. You'll find men who are definitely down on American women because they've been rejected, which puts a whole different complexion on the whole dating issue.

Who Benefits More in Marriage?

WHO BENEFITS MORE FROM MARRIAGE? I am a big romance novel fan, especially the historical fiction. The goal in these tales is for the women to snag the right man to jumpstart their lives. That's why I was shocked when Scarlet O'Hara said, "Marriage, fun? Fiddle-dee-dee. Fun for men you mean."

As a beautiful, wealthy, single woman her responsibilities included little more than dancing, flirting and changing outfits. As a married woman, she would run the household, be the mother, nurse on duty, and social hostess. It was easy to see why Scarlet might not what to give up her lifestyle.

I researched various scholarly journals, surveys, and blogs about marriage to get data. I always assumed women got the better deal. Why else would females scheme in both movies and books to get the man to propose? When women didn't work or have an education, it was beneficial having a man support them. Most women are now self-supporting, making it that much easier to walk away when a marriage doesn't pan out.

Therefore, what are the benefits? I found each sex perceived the other as having all the advantages. The results I managed to cobble together came from **Men's Health** magazine, Dr. Waite (medical doctor), Dr. Porshe Hunt (sociologist), and Dr. Obie Clayton (Sociologist), MSN Money site, and Carolyn Monihan (a blogger.)

Benefits for Men

Helps you live longer

Helps you beat cancer

Keeps you out of trouble

More quality sex

Increases your pay

Speeds up your next promotion/wives support career advancement

Fewer household duties

More happiness

More defined purpose

Being divorced doubles the rate of suicide in men

Married men are more likely to stop smoking

Benefits for Women

Less postpartum depression

Less risk of cardiovascular disease and type 2 diabetes

Less risky behavior

Fewer issues with alcoholism

Companionship

Co-parenting

Dual Benefits

Lower car insurance

Better credit rating

Better loan options

Combined expenses

Shared employer benefits

Increased financial stability

Good mental health

Single people spend twice the amount of time in the hospital as married people do.

I noticed some of the intangible benefits weren't listed, such as when you think you hear someone breaking into the house. When you live alone, you have two choices, investigate or lay awake in fear all night. When married, you wake up your spouse who tells you it's the neighbor or the wind, and you go back to sleep. That might be under good mental health.

I came across a couple of interesting theories in the reading of benefits or lack of them. One was the movies, songs, and books are to get females in a state where they want to get married. If society didn't put the slant for women to get married, then they wouldn't. When a guy doesn't marry, he's a player, but a woman is a rejected loser. Social conditioning determines that.

One commenter put it succinctly by saying the person who benefits is the one who invests the least. We like to believe marriage is an equal partnership, but often there is one person who loves and gives more. The person who loves and does less gets the maximum benefit. The same individual also calls it quits when things don't suit.

As for who benefits the most, I think it depends on the people in the marriage. Personally, I believe I benefit the most in my marriage. Still, I am hoping my husband thinks he benefits the most.

In conclusion, there are other issues that come up in dating, but that's another book. Think about what you want, define your standards, treat yourself with respect and expect others to do likewise. Finally, remember you're out to have fun and just maybe something serendipitous will happen.

www.ingramcontent.com/pod-product-compliance
Lightning Source LLC
Chambersburg PA
CBHW022333280326
41934CB00006B/616